the ART of UKULELE

the ART of UKULELE

An Essential Handbook for Players and Performers

RALPH SHAW

Published by Ralph Shaw
www.ralphshaw.co.uk
RalphShawMusic@gmail.com

Layout and cover design by Setareh Ashrafologhalai
Author photo by Kevin Clark
Part title illustrations by Setareh Ashrafologhalai
Illustration page 129 by Ben Bonham. *Reprinted with permission.*
Editing by Naomi Pauls, Paper Trail Publishing

LIBRARY AND ARCHIVES CANADA CATALOGUING IN PUBLICATION

Shaw, Ralph, 1964–, author
The art of ukulele : an essential handbook for players and performers / Ralph Shaw.

Includes index
ISBN 978-0-9732452-8-8 (paperback)

1. Ukulele—Instruction and study. 2. Ukulele—Performance. I. Title.
MT645.S536 2016 787.8'9193 C2016-902796-1

To Sara Grey, my banjo teacher,
who with kindness and generosity
opened my nineteen-year-old eyes to
the possibility of a musical life.

And to my newsletter readers
for continuing to support my work
and for providing feedback that
entertains me as much as
I hope my writing entertains them.

CONTENTS

III PERFECT YOUR PERFORMANCE

IV LEARN FROM THE GREATS

FOREWORD

JUST KNOWING THAT there are this many aspects to think about in playing and performing with the ukulele makes this book worthwhile.

Ralph is an honest performer who sets out to entertain, and he succeeds! He brings an exceptional brain, amazing energy, lots of experience, quick wit, and a love and respect for people to every performance and to the pages of his books. Not many performers have the unlimited generosity to share their secrets that Ralph has.

Once, someone asked me if I thought that the ukulele was better than the violin. My answer was, "I think all violinists would be better musicians if they also played the ukulele."

Every musician will benefit from knowing Ralph Shaw and reading his new book, *The Art of Ukulele.*

Way to go, Ralph! Another winner!

J. CHALMERS DOANE, OC
November 2015

ANOTHER FOREWORD

'TWAS ONE WEDNESDAY night in 2007 whilst at my local pub, The Huntsman, a small but quaint retreat in South Yorkshire renowned for locally brewed hand-pulled beers, where my eyes beheld an elongated figure of a man entertaining a more-than-ever-before copiously huddled audience. Having witnessed many a band and act within these ancient timbered interiors, I know that the "King of the Ukulele," without any shadow of a doubt, took the night by storm. With his unique interactive comedy, singsong, and a spectacular ukulele performance, he truly captivated the wall-to-wall folk, who in return expressed an overflow of joy on their happy faces.

After the show I was introduced to "Ralph" and we had such a champs chat and chuckle. I must confess that if it weren't for the fact of our meeting that night, I would not have created my own act, *The George Formby Experience*. The idea rooted from Ralph. My uncanny resemblance—like a horse with graveyard teeth—to the British ukulele legend George Formby Jr. was often noted, but I'd always shied away from making use of my God-given appearance. That is, until the pub's landlord, Dave Fields, handed me a ukulele on condition that I make an appearance as "George" with Ralph upon his next visit.

As good as said, as good as done—ask Ralph! (You can read his account on page 171.) I have never looked back since. And for my new fortunes and continuing adventures, I offer my appreciation and praise to dear Ralph, whose influence from the outset paved my own ways and wares. I do urge you readers to see the "King of the Ukulele" live in action if you haven't already done so. Ralph's CDs, I find, are such a delight and are my companion wherever I travel. Eeee by 'eck, and now another book to look forward to. Turned out nice again, hasn't it?

Until we meet again, Ralph, dear chap, God bless and have fun...

PAUL CASPER (A.K.A. GEORGE FORMBY)

BEFORE WE BEGIN: GIVE UP ON GOALS

Where I take issue with our devoutly pro-goal-setting society, where we are expected to be terminally travelling towards worthy targets.

AT FIRST IT seems obvious that we need goals, otherwise nothing would get done, right? But I'm not talking about chores here. On laundry day you're hardly going to stop in the middle of loading the washer to have an existential crisis while you ponder whether the task really needs to be done and consider whether the end result will satisfy the goals and objectives you had in mind when you first took your socks and underwear out of the laundry hamper. No, life is full of those chores we need to do in order to just live. I'm thinking more of the life-goal type of objectives.

I am of the opinion that goal setting is completely unnecessary and that there's way too much of it going on. Goal setting is a concept that enables busy people to become even busier and achieve ever more by assiduously adding more activity into their already over-caffeinated lives. It's a disease.

Indeed, it's a problem that threatens our very survival. Way too many people are getting way too much done in way too short a time. Millions of businesspeople who set financial goals for themselves, their companies and shareholders are causing the obscene plundering of the Earth's finite resources, not to mention damaging the health of good people beyond repair as they are forced to work in lung-searing plastic factories, soul-destroying mines and deadly sweatshops. The very air and water of our planet is being poisoned through the mindless pursuit of someone or other's goals.

People set goals because they see other people getting ahead and moving quicker than they are going. So goal setting is really just a way of pushing harder and faster in order to get a bit closer to the tail ends of the front rats in the great rat race of life.

I have to wonder, how on earth did we manage before goal setting was invented? And when was that exactly? I first became aware of people sticking their goals onto refrigerator doors during the self-help craze of the '80s. Before that nobody I knew ever set a single goal. We just got inspired and then did stuff we liked doing and that was in line with our own personal sense of purpose.

When I was four I sang. At thirteen I found my Uncle Robbie's old harmonica and figured out how to play. At nineteen I learned to play an old banjo I found in the attic. At twenty-one, when my roommate Rob juggled three dice during a Dungeons & Dragons game, I decided to learn to juggle. When I first held a ukulele, I knew it was something I'd do for years to come. When I was twenty-four, I discovered I'd acquired enough weird skills to become an entertainer.

None of these were goals I wanted to achieve; they were all just things I did because (a) they made me feel good; or (b) I felt an urge to do those things. The urge or need to work on a skill is not unlike the need to do chores. Practising an instrument is a sort of chore. If you want to play more cleanly and with self-respect, then you need to practise. But you don't set a goal. That is twisted thinking.

You may wonder, "But Ralph, what harm can there possibly be in setting life goals?" My problem with goals is that they are overly conscious and disconnected intellectual concepts that may be quite inappropriate for our true selves and our individual reality. Attila the Hun was a great goal setter. Just because you *set a goal* to do something doesn't make it right or good.

How can you possibly go within and feel what your soul wishes you to do if you're constantly inventing goals and making your family miserable with your incessant pursuit of objectives? A lot of people have taken up ukulele because they like the idea of doing it; why not, indeed. But if ukulele is not really for you, then you're wasting life's precious hours when you might be better working in a soup kitchen, going hill walking or learning lap dancing. You need to learn what *really* turns your crank. Don't quit ukulele right away, but do figure out what it is you *really* want from it. Get in touch with the inner guide that informs your actions. And until you can do that, you may do best to do nothing. Some timely inaction could be in order, since you won't feel that inner fire if every waking moment is spent being "productive" and "useful."

And don't get me started on bucket lists. What for many is a way of giving meaning to later life is, to me anyway, an idiotic waste of time. So much effort, money and environmental damage spent on shallow experiences in order to tick them off a list. Think of what great soul's purpose you could be missing while you're trudging around crappy old Machu Picchu or hurling yourself off a bridge tied to a bungee or eating snails.

I knew a woman in my Yorkshire village. She was in her nineties and had never travelled more than thirty miles. She never saw Paris or flew in an airplane or watched a bullfight or played ukulele. In fact, now I think of it, I can't remember much of anything interesting she ever did. I just remember the way she talked. So wise and so entertaining—she was awesome. She never lost her luggage.

Lest you doubt me, I know of what I speak. Indeed, I had become so busy that my own inner voice had retreated to little more than a distant bleat. So I decided to slow down and let some things go for a while. I relaxed and took things easier. It was amazing. With all the extra time at my disposal I was able to work on my latest goal, that of completing the book you are about to read. I'm sure glad to tick that little baby off the old bucket list!

So now it's your turn to put your ukulele to one side, sit back, relax and enjoy some inspired ideas to maximize your music.

One

PLAY BETTER UKULELE

THE BEST WAY TO STRUM

A tour of available techniques to help you find your favourite.

I'VE TAUGHT HUNDREDS of strumming workshops. But at the start of each one I always have to go over something very basic: namely, which finger should a strummer use to strum with? I continue to be surprised at the different ways players find to strum. What is completely natural and intuitive to one person feels foreign and uncomfortable to another.

My default strumming method is to use my index finger, but other strummers, most notably many who play Hawaiian music, prefer to play almost exclusively with their thumb. And then I met one student who uses both her index and middle fingers together, and another who uses *all* the fingers of the strumming hand. In Australia I met several players who strum downwards with the index finger and upwards with the thumb. With so many ways to strum (not even considering use of the many picks available), how do we choose which is best?

Let's delve into the different ways you can use your various digits for delivering music.

INDEX FINGER STRUM

Strum with the tip of the index finger and control accuracy by pressing your thumb on the last joint of the index finger. It's as if your finger-end is the pick. Strum down with the back of the nail and strum up with the pad of the finger.

PROS This method enables fast and accurate strumming with a large dynamic range. You'll also find it relatively easy to switch from this strum to other types of strum or individual note picking.

CONS Some people get pain from their finger hitting the strings or the edge of the fretboard. This is especially true for beginners who play overly hard or who haven't developed good accuracy. In some cases damage to the finger and/or fingernail may even occur.

THUMB STRUM

Strum down with the pad of the thumb and up with the thumbnail. After the index finger strum, the thumb strum is probably the second most popular way of strumming.

PROS This is a strum generally favoured by players who like a mellower sound and a slower strum. Instead of strumming with the whole arm, you gain accuracy from using the flexibility of the thumb while the hand, supported by the fingers on the uke body, is held stationary.

CONS It's generally hard to strum loud or fast with the thumb, and I also find it difficult to maintain accuracy when strumming freehand (i.e., strumming with the whole arm). For some of the techniques I teach, such as the syncopated George Formby split stroke or the fast samba, the thumb strum simply cannot keep pace as the tempo picks up speed.

WITH TWO OR MORE FINGERS

Strum down with the fingernails and up with the pads, just like the index finger strum.

PROS This is a great way for people with smaller or weaker fingernails to play. The extra finger surface minimizes pain and finger damage. The technique also allows for louder playing.

CONS When strumming with two or more fingers, it's harder to play quietly.

DOWN WITH THE INDEX, UP WITH THE THUMB

I wasn't really aware of this technique until my recent visit to Australia, where I saw several people using it. I met one teacher, Paul in Sussex Inlet, who recommends this to his beginners as a way to strum that prevents damage to the finger from overly hard and inaccurate strumming.

PROS It's an interesting technique because you get additional control from the action of the index finger flicking down on the down strum and the thumb flicking up on the up strum. The method takes a bit of getting used to, but you may also press the index and thumb together into a single point so that whether you strum down or up, you always have a fingernail making contact with the strings. Another variation is to strum down with index, middle and ring fingers and strum up with the thumb. This makes a sound that is both louder as well as consistent on the up and the down strums.

CONS Like the thumb strum, this technique does not adapt itself easily to faster and more intricate strums.

DOWN WITH THE THUMB, UP WITH THE INDEX

This strum could save your marriage! It comes to me from Susan, who told me her husband liked to use the thumb strum but his thumbnail made an irritating clicking sound on the up strums. To get her to stop wincing, he adapted his strum to down with the thumb and up with the index, and marital bliss ensued.

USE OF PICKS

Rest the pick on the top side of the index finger and hold it in place with the thumb.

PROS A host of different kinds of picks can be purchased. These range from felt picks that make the strum muted and soft to nylon, metal and other materials that provide a louder strum and sharper attack (see page 14). As you can see, picks offer great variation in available sounds. They also prevent pain and damage to fingers.

CONS Picks are easily dropped, which can be inconvenient in the middle of a performance. Keep spares close at hand. Using a pick also makes it harder to switch quickly to finger-playing styles. (Bear in mind that, while it is less common, it is also possible to adopt a hybrid picking style that incorporates both the pick and the remaining fingers of the same hand.)

WHICH STRUM IS BEST?

Would it help if I said all of the above? It's true. If you want your sound to be varied and interesting, then you must vary your strums. Become adept at different playing styles. If you are a thumb strummer, go out of your comfort zone and try using one or more fingers. And if you never use your thumb, try it now; it could add a whole new dimension to your sound.

Spending some time playing in ways that feel strange and foreign can pay off. Benefits include increasing your dynamic range as well as improving your strumming accuracy and your playing speed. The many possible ways of strumming are not limited to the above list. If you have another method that works for you, then go for it.

Ask not what your country can strum for you,
ask what you can strum for your country.
RALPH P. SHAW

IMPROVE YOUR MUSICAL ACCURACY

All about the benefits of getting more exact with your music.

THE SINGLE MOST important thing most of us can do to improve our music is to play with more accuracy. This idea may seem contradictory. Music is an expressive art, so we generally think of celebrating it with freedom, flow and warm, fuzzy feelings, not with a pedantic devotion to precision. In fact, I can already hear you asking, "But Ralph, will attention to more exact playing really improve my music and make it more beautiful to listen to?"

And Ralph says, "Yes, it will. You want to be a good musician? Then be accurate."

The great thing about working on accuracy is that you don't need to learn anything new. Just strive diligently to improve what you're already doing. For example, if you want to work on your singing, then some of the things you can practise include singing every note with exact pitch; making every word clearly understandable; controlling your phrasing, tone, vibrato, and so on.

And when you play ukulele, think about becoming more meticulous in how you play. For example, if there's a difficult chord transition, practise it relentlessly until you land on the strings perfectly and right on time. However, the most noticeable area where we can forever improve our playing is to make each strum happen when it's supposed to. In other words, to play exactly on the beat.

I recently saw an ad in a musicians magazine for a drumbeat analyzer. It helps drummers make their rhythms more exact. The device is a rubber pad that you drum on. The built-in computer then tells you whether your beats arrive early, fall behind or strike right on time. The device appeals to me and I don't know if there is something similar for uke players—probably not. However, a gadget you may already have that can help your playing immensely is the metronome.

Metronome Avoidance Disorder is a disease (I just invented) suffered by quite a few ukulele players, who unfortunately believe that playing to a precise click takes the fun out of playing. If you've tried playing to a metronome and discovered that it's really hard to do, this means you should do more of it, not less. A guaranteed way to make your strumming sound better is to make it more precise. And there's no shortcut to precision other than habituating yourself to a rigorous and regimented beat.

Metronome work is so beneficial because it gets your attention out of yourself, splitting your focus between what you are doing and what is going on around you. It's a great brain exercise. In fact, using the metronome may soon become like a game for you: both fun and challenging at the same time.

Don't worry about overdoing it to the point where your strums become mechanical in their machine-like consistency. That doesn't happen. Enough metronome practice will affect your playing in such a way that most people won't have a clue what you improved. They'll just know they like it better.

So, for a while anyway, instead of learning some new song or technique, try taking what you've got and making it better than ever.

UKE-LESS STRUMMING PRACTICE

Some suggestions to put more variation into your strumming. For this practice you will need a paper bag (or piece of card) and an ability to listen.

It's very common for beginning players to get into a rut with their strumming. After learning the basics, the beginner often adopts a default or one-size-fits-all strum they use for every song. We all know music shouldn't be that way. When we listen to recorded songs we hear each one having a particular feel, or groove, and the essence of that rhythmic feeling, plus the variations within it, is what we want to capture when we strum.

The "feel" of a song refers to the basic quality of a song's rhythm. There are two main types of strumming feel: straight and swing. To illustrate this, pretend to strum a ukulele.

Give the up strums equal value to the down strums so that the timing of your *down-up-down-up* goes: da-da-da-da-da-da-da-da. This is "straight" playing. Now try strumming again. But this time hesitate briefly after each *down* strum so as to make each *up* strum come slightly late. It should sound something like: daa-da-daa-da-daa-da-daa-da. The *down* beats are all right on time, but the *up* beats are a little late. This rhythmic feel is known as "swing."

Most songs we tackle are played either straight or with some degree of swing feel. But as you listen to any recorded piece you'll notice that, as well as the basic feel of a song, other rhythmic nuances can also be added to the mix. So the question becomes: How do we retrain ourselves to strum in new and interesting ways?

I teach many different strumming patterns in *The Complete Ukulele Course* DVD series. But the drawback to teaching specific rhythms is that it's often necessary to get quite analytical, even mathematical, about the structure of each strum. This can be helpful to a point, but a more natural and effective way to develop new strums is simply to listen and copy. And you don't even need a ukulele to do this.

Air strumming could work, but you can improve on it by making your strums audible. One way is to strum the seam of your trouser leg with a pick or a finger while sitting.

Another way is to strum on a paper bag or a piece of light card. If you're using a bag, scrunch up one end and hold it in your left hand while your right hand strums the body of the bag. There's a wonderful old YouTube video of British ukulele entertainer Two-Ton Tessie O'Shea at the Wheeltappers and Shunters Social Club. She uses this technique to great effect as she leads the audience singalong using her paper bag. Alternatively, get a small (playing card–size) piece of flexible card or stiff paper. Hold the card parallel to the floor in your left hand at about the position where your strumming finger makes contact with the strings. Every time you strum, your finger brushes the edge of the card. The card is a good approximation to ukulele strings because as well as audibility, it offers a feel of resistance to the finger.

STEP #1 ***First, just listen.*** And I really mean that. One of the reasons beginners get stuck in the rut of a single strum is that they don't actively listen to what they are strumming along with. Put all your focus into listening to the rhythm and beats of the music. When you feel ready, then and only then, pick up your paper bag or piece of card and start to strum along.

STEP #2 ***Get the feel.*** While still listening, allow your finger to strum your paper to match the feel of the song. Focus on the listening, and let your strumming hand discover its own way to find the groove of the music. The feel may be swing or be played straight—or be mostly straight with perhaps a flavour of swing in it. Any combination is possible. Let your innate musicality find the rhythm. If you find there are too many rhythmic elements within the music to fit your strum, try doubling the strumming speed and see if that helps.

STEP #3 ***Put in extra beats, missing beats and other variations.*** Once you've settled into the feel of the song, it's now time to add or remove any other beats you can hear. There's no rule for exactly how to go about this. Keep listening to the rhythm section—usually drums, bass, piano, guitar, but there could be other instruments too. Remain intent on the listening while you allow your finger to put in extra accents (more pronounced strums) or miss out certain beats altogether by deliberately missing the paper on the beats you don't want to hear. Then take it a step further: Include variations to the basic strum while still being faithful to the song's feel.

Using a paper bag or cardboard rectangle in this way removes us from all the parts of ukulele playing that aren't related to strumming. It helps us to break old, unhelpful patterns while creating new ways to play.

And, should you arrive at your gig to discover you left your instrument at home, you can always take a tip from the great Tessie O'Shea and entertain the audience using only a paper bag. Who knows, they might enjoy it even more than your uke playing!

PICKING YOUR UKULELE

Using a pick to play ukulele can change your sound, and you have several types of picks to choose from.

BACK IN 1990 when I started playing ukulele I was told, by everyone who knew anything about ukulele, that I'd need to get a felt pick to strum with. I never questioned this advice and spent a good couple of years using a felt pick. And I don't regret it either. My granddad used one back in the 1920s. It's a chunky little chappie that's easy to grip and flail away at your strings with, and it does so without your fingers getting hurt: a bonus for beginners who want to develop their strumming technique and chording without the misery of torn cuticles.

But generally, picking, plucking and strumming using your fingers and thumb is the superior way to play, as it offers a greater variety of sounds than can be achieved with a single pick. That said, picks are cheap and they may have a surprising effect on your sound that could benefit certain songs or parts of songs, so I would definitely encourage you to try some out.

Some ukulele purists respond negatively to the idea of playing ukulele with a pick. But exactly *how* an instrument is played shouldn't matter. Music is about sound, so whether you use a finger, a thumb, a pick or boxing gloves, it's all in the choice of the musician.

Here are my thoughts on some picks that I have tried or heard about over the years:

- ***Large felt pick.*** This is the one mentioned above. Approximately 2 inches long and ¼ inch thick, it emulates the action of a strumming finger. It's great for beginners because it's easy to keep hold of. Get one that's as stiff as possible but with a little flex to it. Avoid felt picks that are too weak and pliable.
- ***Small felt pick.*** Useful for soft picking, where the attack of a hard plastic pick is somewhat harsh.
- ***Jim Dunlop USA Nylon .60mm grey pick.*** I like these picks because they are cheap, have a sound I like, never break and are available everywhere. Their textured grip also makes them easy to hold. I've used these picks for years. However, I find them slightly too pointy, so whenever I buy a new one I trim the point with nail scissors and a file to make it more rounded. These picks are great for making your uke strumming noticeably louder. You gain volume and a sharper attack but lose the softness that finger-playing gives.

- ***Moshay nylon pick.*** These are a handmade, more expensive cousin of the above. They have a nice hole in the middle to aid grip or for tying a string through. They are slightly more flexible and therefore kinder on the face of your instrument.
- ***Small plastic guitar pick.*** I've never been happy with these for strumming. They are harder to keep hold of and eventually crack and break. They can be good for melody picking though.
- ***Larger plastic guitar pick.*** I've often seen uke players use these for melody picking. They are easier to hold onto than small picks (and easier to find when you drop them).
- ***Felt-plastic-felt sandwich pick.*** Personally I'm not a fan of these, as the felt part of the sandwich seems to wear out quickly. Thus you soon lose the softer felt sound and end up with more of the clack of the plastic.
- ***Fingerpicks.*** Fingerpicks are usually made from steel or plastic and are great if you're a skilled player. They make every note sound loud and clear, but beware that they highlight your mistakes too. For most beginners I would not recommend them and instead suggest using your fingers to pick the strings. But if you want to see how fingerpicks can really be used to great effect, do check out the work of resophonic ukulele maestro (or is it maestress?) Del Rey of Seattle.

I asked other uke players for comments about picks. Here's what I got:

- Leather picks are "easy on strings and instrument."
- Fred Kelly picks come in a variety of designs. The company uses a Delrin material that "is far less harsh in sound and sounds much like a fingernail. In fact, the Delrin material is easier on strings and soundboards than fingernails."
- "I've been using a coconut shell pick I made a long time ago. It is rounded more like some of the jazz guitar picks and is not as brittle sounding as some of the plastic picks I've used when I need volume and articulation."

- "Have you tried the rubber picks? I carry one made by Wedgie (3.1mm). They are quite popular among pick users because they're flexible and easy to hold. I think they can also be used for bass."
- "I put the pickguard on all my most loved ukes. It really helps minimize damage from picks. I also wanted to mention the ZeroGravity picks for players who have trouble gripping like I do (from a swollen right hand due to surgery)."

FIVE WAYS TO INCREASE YOUR MUSICAL WILLPOWER

Where there's a will there's a won't, so herewith some suggestions to keep up with practice when you don't feel like it.

ONE SUMMER I took time off from writing. I did so because I was lacking a certain quality that is well known to musicians: the much sought after, elusive force known as willpower. It shouldn't be a big deal. After all, summer is traditionally a time to kick back and slack off. But the truth is, I had no will to write. In fact, the only reason I ended up writing the piece you're reading now is that my self-analytical side, while pondering my own lack of will, caught its own tail and became strangely motivated to write a piece about willpower.

My lack of drive came from being unusually busy for about ten months. In that time I recorded two albums, organized and fulfilled a US west coast tour and put on a CD release concert. Those few words quickly sum up what I'd done, but they don't do justice to the exponential number of tasks required to make each of those things happen: making decisions, sending emails, second-guessing my decisions, fundraising, organizing rehearsals, chasing good ideas that went nowhere, dealing with illnesses (though not mine) and planning advertising. And that list doesn't include family and other emergencies that got thrown into the mix just for added excitement. Such is life for the DIY musician. Much of the process was enjoyable, but there are large parts of the work I find both stressful and tedious. So when people say, "Oh, you sing and play ukulele for a living. How fun! That must be nice and relaxing," all I can do is laugh sardonically and with bitter contempt.

All this is to say that when my intense work period finally ended, I found myself feeling pretty burnt out and devoid of that inner motivating force we call willpower. Groucho Marx called it *won't* power. When Groucho was in his seventies, his doctor allowed the sweet-toothed comedian only two candies a day. After eating his daily allowance, Groucho would turn to his assistant and say, "Nothing left to do now but wait for tomorrow."

How do we find the strength to strum when our get-up-and-go has gone? Here are some ideas to resuscitate your willpower.

USE THE THRILL TO GIVE YOU WILL

When you get a new instrument, it's a thrill to sit down and practise. You're excited to play. I am often reminded of this by newer players, who describe their interest in ukulele as an obsession. They refer to themselves as uke-aholics. As in, "Hi, I'm so-and-so and I'm a uke-aholic!" Ha-ha!

If there is a place for addiction to be glorified, then this could be it. For it's a wonderful time. Use that feeling to motivate yourself. Don't assume you'll have this inner drive forever, because chances are you won't. The time will inevitably come when you discover the desire to pick up and play your instrument has diminished. So ride your enthusiasm like a kid on a carnival ride who wants to go again and again. Harness the joy you feel and let it propel your practice and your playing.

PLAY DAILY

When the will has gone, musicians use their daily practice routine to keep the fire alive. Daily engagement with your instrument brings regular moments of success. It's exciting to play something you couldn't play yesterday, and this return on your investment makes you want to play more. In music, getting better is its own reward. Also scientists have shown that your amount of daily willpower is a finite resource. So make your music a priority, or you may lose it to less worthy activities.

REMEMBER THE GOOD TIMES

I recently had a chance encounter with someone who recognized me from a performance. His face beamed as he recalled how much he'd enjoyed the show. He even remembered a specific song (the George Formby classic "Auntie Maggie's Remedy") and told me he was thrilled to meet me. His positive support was an absolute tonic for me—a reminder of why I practise. His face recalled how my audiences look when the show goes great as well as how that makes me feel inside. It made me want to run home and practise.

KEEP IT FUN

I've been playing ukulele since 1990. It would be odd to bounce around with the enthusiasm of a beginner at this point. That is one reason I love to run my ukulele club, the Vancouver Ukulele Circle. Once a month I get to be in a concert hall with over a hundred new strummers, and their enthusiasm is infectious. In fact, just two nights ago we came together for two and a half hours of song, laughter and fun. Maybe that's why I woke up feeling so motivated to write today.

BE NICE TO YOU

Go easy on yourself. Occasionally it's good to just take a break. Use your mind and body in different ways so you can return fresh to your practice later. But set a time limit for your break, so you'll be mentally prepared for the day your playing goes back into high gear again.

KEEPING IT STRAIGHT—YOUR WRIST, THAT IS

A brief lesson on why it's important to keep your non-strumming wrist fairly straight when you play.

I OFTEN SEE UKULELE players holding their ukulele neck with their wrist (that's the left wrist for right-handed players) at a very sharp angle. I can only assume that at some point they decided it was easier or more comfortable to do so. I used to be one of those people. For many years I was quite oblivious to how I was holding my ukulele neck. That is, until a guitar-playing friend of mine gave me a very simple demonstration that illustrated the importance of keeping a straight wrist. Try it and you'll see what I mean.

Hold your hand up in front of you with your wrist nice and straight. Now wiggle your fingers as fast as you can. Done that? Excellent! Now do it again, but this time bend your wrist sharply so your hand is 90 degrees to your forearm (it doesn't matter which direction you bend). Wiggle your fingers as fast as you can. Do you notice the difference?

The fingers move with far greater ease and efficiency if your wrist is straight.

But I am not saying you must keep this wrist straight and rigid when you play. Allow it to flex both forward and back. On average, however, aim to develop a habit of keeping a more or less straight wrist.

IT'S ALL RIGHT BEING LEFT-HANDED

Thoughts and tips for the 10 percent: left-handed musicians who manage to play music in a right-handed world.

CONSIDER THE UNUSUAL case of rock guitarist Jimi Hendrix. He was born left-handed but, as was common in those days, was forced to write with his right hand. When young Jimi got his first guitar, it was strung for a right-handed player. His father, a somewhat superstitious type, believed that doing anything left-handed was the work of the Devil, so Jimi learned to play right-handed. But he also discovered that by flipping the guitar over he could play it upside down in left-handed fashion—with the bass strings towards the floor. Of course, to prevent his guitar being taken away, he'd be quick to flip it back to right-handed style should his father suddenly walk into the room.

Eventually, and no longer under fatherly control, Jimi got himself a guitar strung for left-handed playing. But by then his ambidextrous ability was so well developed that he was able to also flip it over and play upside down in right-handed style.

It's hard not to believe that Jimi's unusual upbringing somehow magnified his musical mind. Learning to play his instrument in all these different ways can only have multiplied the neuron connections in his brain and may even have been the catalyst for his genius. But what I take from his story is that being left handed in a right-handed world is not necessarily a disadvantage. Depending on how the left-handed player deals with their role as a southpaw strummer, the resulting music may have special qualities not normally heard in right-handed music.

If you are left-handed and starting out on ukulele, here are some things to bear in mind.

CONSIDER LEARNING ON A RIGHT-HANDED INSTRUMENT

An experienced guitar teacher told me that when one is first learning a stringed instrument, both hands have a lot of new skills to acquire. And for a left-hander to gain these skills on a right-handed instrument can have big advantages in the future. In social settings where an instrument happens to be lying around, it is far more likely to be made for a right-handed player. A person able to play such an instrument is at a greater advantage than someone having to depend on playing a left-handed instrument. The teacher also pointed out that she has never known a left-handed student to regret having learned on a right-handed instrument.

FLIP A RIGHT-HANDED INSTRUMENT OVER

One way to strum with the left hand while playing a standard right-handed instrument is to flip the instrument over so that the strings are all upside down. Try it sometime—it feels pretty weird. Musician Ian Whitcomb was the first person I ever saw play in this way. It seems very unintuitive at first. But whereas some chords become harder to play, others are now easier, so ultimately this form of playing balances out.

GET A LEFT-HANDED INSTRUMENT

My friend Tom Saunders is a gifted left-handed performer who regularly performs and leads songs at Vancouver Ukulele Circle meetings. He had quite a bit to tell me about left-handed ukuleles. For one thing, instrument makers clearly prefer making right-handed instruments. You'll be lucky to find even 5 percent of a store's inventory as left-handed instruments.

Fortunately, if the ukulele's body shape is symmetrical, it's a simple matter to reverse the strings. Having high strings on both top and bottom makes this especially easy, because the slots in the nut and the bridge will still match the string thicknesses. However, if you play with a low 4th string (that's the G for GCEA players), you may have problems flipping the strings since a fat string may not go into a narrow slot and, at the other side, a narrow string in a wide slot may create buzzing. So it may be necessary to change both the nut and the bridge—a fairly simple job for a luthier.

You'll also discover that you no longer have dots on the edge of the neck to show where to put your fingers. You can either draw some on yourself or get your luthier to do a more professional-looking job.

An instrument with a cutaway is a problem. A cutaway is the modified body shape that enables you to reach the highest notes on the neck. When the instrument is flipped upside down, the cutaway is unhelpfully now on top. Similarly when converting an electric right-handed ukulele, you'll probably find that the positions of knobs on the body are now in the way of your strumming hand. Also the jack to plug in your cord is now on top instead of underneath. This can also be altered by a luthier if necessary.

LEARN TO READ CHORD BOXES BACKWARDS

Tom tells me that the chord boxes in ukulele sheet music are all backwards to left-handers, but he has become used to reading them the opposite way. The ability to read chord boxes is itself a somewhat abstract mental technique, so if you can already do that, it won't be an insurmountable feat to retrain yourself to read them in a new way.

WHAT ABOUT ADVANTAGES?

Despite my initial comments, there don't seem to be too many pluses for the lefty ten-percenters. But here's one. Tom says, "I actually find it easier to tell what chords a right-handed player is playing than a left-handed player, as it's a direct mirror image to me—so that's one good thing out of a hundred!"

HOW TO DO THE ONE-FINGER ROLL

Instructions for playing a roll on a ukulele, including an attempt to describe the most economical technique of all.

ONE OF THE great benefits of not using a pick is having your fingers and thumb available. This gives you access to a wider variety of playing techniques. One such technique is the roll. A roll is what you hear when several individual beats happen so quickly that you hear a continuous vibrating sound. For example, if you flick through a deck of playing cards slowly, you'll hear *flak-flak-flak*. But do it quickly and you'll hear something more like *fl-r-r-r-r-r-r-r-r* (the rolling *r-r-r-r* sound being like the front-of-tongue vibration of the *r* when a Spaniard says *burro*).

The roll is also one of the signature sounds of Spanish flamenco guitar. The sound is achieved by strumming down on the strings, one finger at a time, using some or all fingers of the strumming hand. You can try it right now. Find a level surface and drum the pads of your fingers on it as if you were impatiently waiting for something. Try using three fingers. Do it slowly at first, making sure to keep all the beats evenly spaced. Speed up the roll. Now add another finger and then the thumb, so all five digits are making a nice "thrumming" sound. Now reverse it: if you began the roll with your pinky, now start it using the thumb.

Playing a roll on the ukulele is very similar to drumming on a desk, except that instead of using the pads of the fingers, you'll more likely be using the fingernails or sides of the fingers. Experiment with the three- and four-finger roll. Always aim for a clear rolling sound and incorporate it into your playing. I show the technique on two of my DVDs: *The Complete Ukulele Course* and *Essential Strums for the Ukulele.*

Most players favour starting a three- or four- finger roll with the pinky finger. Others, like myself, begin the roll using the index finger and end with the ring or pinky finger. The former method has the advantage that it allows you to do a five-finger roll, ending with the thumb, if you so wish.

Ever heard of the six-finger roll? It sounds like the start to a joke, but it actually is a real technique. I first heard of it being taught by Bob Brozman. It involves changing the direction of the roll so that one or more fingers are being used more than once in a seamlessly continuous sound. This leads us to the highly improbable but very real ten-finger roll! Matt Dahlberg showed me this extraordinary technique. It involves the five digits rolling first in one direction and then immediately rolling back the other way. The slinky movement of the hand makes me think of a double helix. The ten-finger roll sounds exciting and is visually stunning but musically pretty useless. Even Matt admits that the technique, though highly cool, is not one that fits comfortably into most musical situations.

Myself, I prefer simpler techniques. You can get an excellent roll by having the index finger strum down immediately followed by the thumb.

This *thumb roll* is shown in the syncopated strum section of my *Essential Strums* DVD.

But for sheer simplicity, nothing can beat the one-finger roll. This is an unusual technique. My usual policy is to instruct learners to practise new techniques slowly before gradually building up speed. Unfortunately, I find that the one-finger roll only truly sounds like a roll when played at speed. So you have to figure it out on the fly. Also note that it is effective if you strum with your finger-end like I do. But it may not work for thumb strummers.

Start by playing one of your faster numbers. As you strum, put in a quick shake of the finger and then return to the regular strum. That's all there is to it. Technically what you're doing is inserting a very short and fast tremolo. Keep a nice loose wrist as you strum down-up-down-up and then quickly add some additional down-ups at double speed. But it is far easier to simply think of this method as incorporating an added finger-shake.

A bonus of this technique is that if you do happen to strum with a pick, you can now play a roll using only the pick, without having to use any additional fingers.

WHAT'S THE NEXT CHORD? PART I: CHORDS AT YOUR FINGERTIPS

Five handy tips to help you remember chords and chord progressions.

PAM, ONE OF my newsletter readers, once asked me: "I have no trouble memorizing words and melody, but I find myself lost when it comes to playing the correct chord from memory. Is it a matter of instinct—knowing the right chord progressions? Or maybe just spending more time practising without the page? Could it be age-related? Sheer distraction or nerves?"

This is a great question for which there are several answers. Here is part 1.

When I was a first-year physics undergraduate, we had a senior lecturer whom we called "King Richard" (he got this name because his grey hair was cut in a medieval style much in vogue with knights of yore). As well as a peculiar haircut, he had two teaching habits worthy of mention. One was to use the word "recipe" for every mathematical proof he ever wrote on the blackboard. His goal in this regard was to get us to realize that any mathematical formula, no matter how complex, was simply a means to an end. In other words, following the formula will lead the student to the correct conclusion as surely as following a baking recipe will help turn out a perfect chocolate cake. It's a good lesson. Any major task seems less onerous if we can switch our thinking about it.

However, he said "recipe" a *lot.* The word came out of his mouth so often that we invented the Recipe Game. Every time King Richard said the word "recipe," you had to scratch your head. If you missed one, you had to scratch three times. My physics pals and I resembled a line of chimpanzees in the middle of the classroom. *Recipes* were coming thick and fast as we simultaneously scribbled formulas, scratched our heads and suppressed a gradually mounting hysteria.

This story reveals several things about me, including why I loved physics, why I was no good at it and why I have scant hair on the sides of my head. King Richard's other habit was to regularly insist that certain equations should always be *at our fingertips.* It was an ever-present reminder that some categories of knowledge shouldn't require thought, research or googling. We should just *know* them. And it's true; to be a successful ukulele entertainer, your chord changes need to be *at your fingertips.*

A good song performance requires that the words and chords be so ingrained within the mind-body memory that minimal effort is needed to recall them. But as Pam—the writer of the above question—has discovered, learning lyrics often comes more easily than memorizing chords.

One reason for this is our ability to run lyrics and melodies in our mind at any time of day, even while running errands and pursuing other non-ukulele activities. Unfortunately, without a ukulele in our hand, the chord changes tend to go unpractised at these times, so extra work needs to be done. Here are some practical tips to get those chord changes into your fingertips.

TIP #1 ***Focus on just the chords.*** Sit down with the ukulele and play a song through while just focusing on the chords. Ignore the words and the tune as much as possible. If you don't happen to have a ukulele to hand, then mentally go over the chord changes in much the same way as you run lyrics in your mind. Visualize where your fingers would go.

TIP #2 ***Look for patterns of chords.*** Most songs have repeating chord patterns. Find where these repeating sequences are and where the patterns break down. For example, most standard songs of the jazz, pop and swing eras have four parts typically of eight measures each. The first, second and fourth parts share close to identical chord patterns. However, the chord grouping in the third section tends to be completely different to the other three parts. Therefore, playing the song through once gives us three times more practice on the chord grouping found in parts 1, 2 and 4 than on the chords in section 3. So it's wise to isolate the underplayed section and practise it more to bring it to the level of the rest of the song.

TIP #3 ***Sing the chord names as you play.*** Doing this will aid memorization. It also helps you to connect the sound of chords to the part of the brain that remembers chord names. This proves useful when writing songs, jamming or needing to come up with chords for yourself at any other time.

TIP #4 ***Play at high speed.*** We should always look for ways to make practice fun. Here's a way to do that. Once you think you know a song, try playing it as fast as you possibly can. Forget about sounding nice; this is just to get you covering as many chords as possible in the shortest amount of time. As well as being good exercise for your strumming arm, this technique also helps you to pinpoint the areas of the song where you need to slow down and do more work.

TIP #5 ***Start at the end.*** When practising there's a tendency to commence each song from the beginning. Then, if we get interrupted, we start over from the beginning again. Ultimately this means that the first half of a song gets a lot more attention than the second half. So try working on the last quarter of a song first, then the last half, then the last three quarters, and finally play the song from the start. Practising in this way also gets us used to the idea of dropping into a song in the middle—a useful skill to have when playing with others.

Memorizing chords may seem daunting now, but in time you'll discover that, by following the above recipe (*scratch-scratch*), whenever a chord change comes your fingertips will automatically know where to go.

WHAT'S THE NEXT CHORD? PART 2: HITTING THE PERCENTAGES

How to improve your chances of scoring the musical equivalent of goals and hit the right chords when jamming with others.

JOCKS ARE GOOD at sport: they hit harder, throw balls farther and score more love interests. I was never one of the school jocks. Mine was a somewhat tough school, and I was no good at skills like running, jumping, throwing and kicking. And that was just the chess club.

Later in life I was surprised to discover *musical* jocks: the ones who manage to play something impressive no matter what gets thrown at them. If you've ever floundered around in a jam session, perhaps spending most of every song trying to figure out what key everyone's in, you'll know the people I'm talking about: arpeggio athletes who always figure out the key and chords in no time at all. You wonder, "How do they do that?"

Some spent years studying music. They did all the hard slog that most of us thought we could avoid by playing ukulele. Not having benefited from such an education, I've instead acquired a somewhat incomplete knowledge of chords to the point where I can now make, shall we say, *un*-educated guesses about what chords are coming next. And just like the jocks, who are always looking to improve their percentages in terms of hits, runs, goals, and so on, I look to increase my chances of landing on correct chords when I'm jamming with others. Here are some tips to help you do that.

TIP #1 ***Find the key everyone is playing in.*** This is challenging but gets easier the more you do it. Try to find the single note that most fits with the song. If a song is in the key of C, then C will generally be the last note and the last chord. In most jams the songs tend to be in the keys of C, F, G, D, A and B-flat, so try those notes first. When the key note (or root note) is played repeatedly through a song, it fits the song better than any other note.

An obvious way to figure out the key is to ask someone. However, this doesn't always work; others may be even more confused than you are. It's also possible that they are one of the special breed of (usually) old-timers who play according to finger shapes and have no idea what the names of the chords actually are. So check people's chord fingering. If you notice C, F and G7 chords are being played a lot, then you can pretty well bet that the song is in C. Similarly F, B-flat and C7 point to the key of F, and so on for other keys.

But watch out for minor keys! For example, if you're fairly sure that the root note is D but the chords D, G and A don't sound right, it could be that D-minor is the key and the chords D-minor, G-minor and A will work better.

To expand on this idea, play these chords: C, D-minor, E-minor, F, G, A-minor, B-diminished, C. You can actually hear the C scale, right? These are the characteristic chords that help you know you're either in C or A-minor. This is a useful framework for figuring out the chords in a particular key. (Note: This doesn't give a full picture since it fails to account for seven chords and for the fact that composers, ignoring musical rules, often put in other chords that sound cool but aren't in the same key.)

TIP #2 ***Notice the song style.*** Certain song styles have predefined structures that help when figuring out chords. A blues song in C, for example, generally has the chords C, F and G (or G7), and you need to listen only a few times to know exactly where those changes happen. Traditional folk songs also use those same three chords plus an occasional minor chord, such as A-minor or E-minor. The chords can come in any order, so look at some songs and notice common chord patterns. Modern songs—from the past few decades—often use the I, V, VI, IV chord progression. (Those Roman numerals correspond to the characteristic chords mentioned above. In the key of C they are: I = C , II = D-minor, III = E-minor, IV = F, V = G, VI = A-minor, VII = B-diminished, VIII = C.)

The I, V, VI, IV chord progression (for the key of C = C, G, A-minor, F) has been found to produce the greatest emotional impact in human beings in our western society (and believe me, the music business is well aware of this fact). Part of the emotional appeal of Bruddha Iz's "Over the Rainbow" is due to this chord progression. If you want further proof of this, visit YouTube to see a hilarious medley by the Australian comedy group the Axis of Awesome. It's in the key of E, and if you want to play along, the chords are E, B, C-sharp-minor and A.

TIP #3 ***Learn the circle of fifths.*** Songs from the pre–rock 'n' roll era (jazz, swing and Tin Pan Alley–type songs) often use many more chords than those described above and are harder to figure out by ear. But this is where the "circle of fifths" diagram that you often see in music tuition books can come in handy. Look at any song in the key of C. You'll notice the last chord of the song is C and the one prior to it is almost always G7. That G7 chord leaves us with a feeling of hanging. And then when we play the C chord, it's with a feeling of landing. In music theory G is known as the fifth of C. Count on your fingers starting with C as the thumb. D is the index, E is the middle finger, F is the ring finger and G is the fifth finger.

Do this again with G as the thumb. Count up from G and you now find that D, the pinky, is the fifth note. Repeat this with D as the thumb and you discover that A is the fifth of D. E is the fifth of A, and so on. (You don't have to use your fingers, but it helps me!) Many songs use the sequence of fifths, and knowing this can help a lot. Take the song "Five Foot Two, Eyes of Blue." The chords go C, E7, A7, D7, G7, C. You can see it's all fifths: E is the fifth of A, A is the fifth of D, D is the fifth of G, G is the fifth of C. Not all songs have such a nice string of fifths, but if a song is in C and everyone's playing an A7, it's a good bet the next chord will be D7, the one after that G7 and then C.

TIP #4 ***Practise transposing into other keys.*** As you work through the above chord changes in the key of C, you also need to transfer what you've learned into other common keys. For example, take a three- or four-chord song that you always play in C and play it in the key of F. Now try it in other keys, such as G, A, D and B-flat. Get used to doing this and you'll notice the difference next time you are jamming.

Even a full understanding of all the above will not guarantee that you always find the right chord. But your chances of success will increase as you gain experience. Perhaps from time to time you'll play a string of correct chords—the musical equivalent of scoring a goal or hitting a home run—and what a great feeling that will be.

PLAY LIKE AN OLD-TIMER

A certain type of player can play any song in any key. How do they do that?

BEA BLACKWELL PLAYED piano in the Billy Bishop Royal Canadian Legion hall on the west side of Vancouver every Friday night for more than three decades. She had a vast repertoire of singalong favourites from the world war eras and Hollywood musicals. Showing up with my banjo uke, I needed to tell her only the name of a song and then start playing. She'd nod her head as her fingers travelled across the ivories, poking at certain piano keys to find the key in which I was playing. Seconds later both her hands would be in full flow, driving the honky-tonk machine in a forceful, striding style.

I've met other musicians of Bea's generation who play ukulele like she plays piano. All of them share the following characteristics: they were born in the 1920s, they can seemingly play anything, and they claim not to read music. Growing up in a time when recording was in its infancy and radio was the latest techno marvel, some kids had lots of time on their hands. A musically curious child had endless hours to unravel the mystery of any instrument that came their way. The result was an enviable ease and facility with their instrument that is so very different from how most people play today.

Like most things that look simple, but are hard to do, the art of playing any song in any key is several skills stitched together to appear as one ability. I still consider myself a novice at this, but with the right knowledge and years of playing, you too will be able to play ukulele like an old-timer. In fact, by then there's a good chance you actually will be an old-timer.

To get to this place, you will need to:

1. Figure out the key of any song you hear.
2. Think of chords as finger shapes instead of names and play barre chords effortlessly.

3. Know the chord changes of hundreds of songs and/or be able to recognize common chord patterns.

1. FIND THE RIGHT KEY

Go to YouTube, or put on some CDs, and just go from song to song figuring out the key for each. The last note of a song usually tells you the key, and there are other techniques too (see previous chapter). Finding the key is a skill that develops the more you do it.

2. THINK OF CHORDS AS FINGER SHAPES

To play a song in any key, on a GCEA-tuned ukulele, you need to know it only in the keys of C, F and B-flat. (For ukes tuned A D F-sharp B, the keys you need to be fluent in are D, G and C. For ukes tuned DGBE, the three keys are G, C and F. But from here on I'll only be giving chord names for GCEA tuning.)

Key of C: Play a simple three-chord song in C. Say, "King of the Road" or "Jamaica Farewell." Use the chords C, F and G7. To change this song to the key of C-sharp, begin by making a barre at the first fret. (Barre means to press your index finger down across all four strings at a particular fret.) Now, while barreing, play exactly the same shapes for C, F and G7 as you did before. You're now playing the song a semitone higher. Move your barreing index finger to the next fret and play those chord shapes again. The song is now in D, a whole tone higher. Continue up the neck playing the song in ever rising keys. You find that knowing the name of each individual chord is no longer much of a help. It's actually simpler to just think of them as finger shapes. As you continue up the fretboard the sound gets progressively more plinky, so let's change and play the song in the key of F.

Key of F: In the key of F, the chords for our three-chord song are now F, B-flat and C7. Once you can play the song with these chords, move them all up by a semitone, once again barreing at the first fret and playing the same chord shapes. The chords are now called F-sharp, B and C-sharp7 although, as I said before, you don't need to know those names, just their shapes. Keeping these same finger shapes, you can play the song in different keys by moving the shapes up and down the fretboard. But should you find that neither of the C or F chord groups is giving you the desired results, then try switching to the key of B-flat.

Key of B-flat: The chord names for our same three-chord song are now B-flat, E-flat and F7. As before, once you're familiar with these shapes, you can play in different keys by moving them to different places on the fretboard using a barre.

Understanding the above, we realize we can play our three-chord song in any key. It's a wonderful concept. You may discover that moving quickly through these chord shapes and taking them up the fretboard also gives you an additional tool in locating the key of any song.

Let's now move from a three-chord song to one that has four or five chords. In the key of C, a five-chord song may have the chords C, F, G, A-minor and D7. Make a barre and play the song in different places along the neck. Now transpose the song to the key of F (so C becomes F, F becomes B-flat, G7 becomes C7, A-minor becomes D-minor and D7 becomes G7). Again, with your barre, play the song in different places up and down the fretboard. Got the hang of that? Then do the same song again in the key of B-flat (so F becomes B-flat, B-flat becomes E-flat, C7 becomes F7, D-minor becomes G-minor, and G7 becomes C7).

If you are new to transposing, then the above may have you scratching your head in bewilderment. Transposing is actually not that hard. It's merely a fancy word for changing all the chords or notes in a song by the same amount.

Once you can play all your songs in the keys of C, F and B-flat, and can move them up and down the ukulele neck, you are there. With those three chord sets, you'll be able to play in any key without necessarily having to know the names of every single chord you're playing.

3. LEARN SONGS AND CHORD PATTERNS

Now learn a whole pile of songs and learn them in those three chord positions. As you do this, you'll become familiar with chord patterns that get used over and over again in popular, folk, jazz, blues and classical music. The important thing is that for each song you learn in the key of F, for example, make sure you also learn it in C and B-flat. Obviously this can take a while. So if you wish to become one of those old-timers who can play any song in any key, I suggest you get started right away.

SEVEN TIPS TO MAKE YOU WANT TO PRACTISE

If you're feeling the need to revive your daily music practice habit, here are some ideas to get back into it.

THE STUDENTS AT James Hill's annual weekend of ukulele workshops in Langley, BC, in 2014 had an opportunity to quiz the teachers (Chalmers Doane, Hélène Beaulieau, Paul Luongo, Aaron Keim, Kevin Carroll and myself) on any ukulele-related issues they had in mind. One student asked for a practice tip from each teacher. Here is some of what was said.

TIP #1 ***Practise for one minute—every day.*** This is a favourite tip from Chalmers Doane. All you have to do is commit to practising for one minute every day (including Christmas and statutory holidays). The only rule is that it be a full minute of concentrated and focused practice. No daydreaming! And the one minute begins *after* the ukulele is removed from its case. Afterwards you may choose to continue practising for longer than a minute. But that is up to you.

TIP #2 ***Keep it fun.*** Remember it is called *playing* the ukulele. So make your practice time enjoyable and playful. For example, think of your scales as games. Find different ways to play them by changing the timing and the order of the notes. Also reward yourself with music and songs that pique your interest and make you want to play them often.

TIP #3 ***Really listen to your instrument.*** This tip came from Hélène Beaulieau. When you pick up your ukulele, instead of getting straight on with the business of playing, just strum the open strings and pay close attention to the sound. Truly listen. How do you feel? What does the sound do to your senses? Think about sound. Remember that practice is not about creating physical movements; it is about making sound.

TIP #4 ***Any time can be practice time, so keep your instrument within easy reach.*** I wouldn't necessarily suggest this for trumpet, timpani, double bass or bagpipes, all of which require a dedicated practice space. But ukuleles are distinctive in that they can be transported anywhere and played at low volume in kitchen, car, bedroom, living room or waiting room without causing too much offence.

TIP #5 ***Get a good instrument.*** Having a freshly strung ukulele that gives you a great feeling just to hold and hear it will make a huge difference. The pleasure of a well-made and great-sounding instrument can only inspire you to want to spend more time with it.

TIP #6 ***Practise with performance in mind.*** Some people play music purely for personal recreation, but most of us plan at some time to share our music with others. Practising for performance can mean many things. It can raise the quality of your singing and playing to a higher level. Practising as if an audience is watching can help you become familiar with playing outside of your comfort zone. Make sure to become adept at the trickier parts of songs to prevent your playing from falling apart in those places. Working towards a goal of putting the song across to an audience will deepen your connection to the instrument and to your music.

TIP #7 ***Consider the future if you fail to practise now.*** Here is a slightly sad personal story. In 2002 I bought a white upright piano. My goal was for both my daughter and myself to learn to play. I imagined a future where our home would be filled with boogie-woogie, ragtime and singalong parties. But over time my daughter gave up her lessons and I simply neglected to play the instrument. And there it stands to this day, untouched and unplayed. And this next part may make me sound a little crazy, but I feel sorry for the piano. I imagine it came to our home feeling as I did at the time: excited and eagerly anticipating the music it would be making. Instead it has become a forlorn feature of our household furniture: a despondent repository for old books and bric-a-brac that get loaded onto its sad little lid. For most of these years it has stood silent, yearning to be played.

So if you won't practise for *you*, at least do it for the sake of your instrument.

HOW MUCH SHOULD WE PUSH OUR KIDS?

Ways we can turn our children into musicians without resorting to the yardstick.

IN THE "WHO really wrote Shakespeare?" debate, some say William Shakespeare could not have written the works attributed to him. And you do have to wonder how the lowly son of a glover could have written in such knowing detail about English (and Danish) royalty, Italian nobility and other cultural goings-on that he could not have experienced first-hand.

But the most damning piece of evidence that Shakespeare did not write Shakespeare is the fact that his children were functionally illiterate. Really, how could that be? Shakespeare's vocabulary was immense. As well, he invented the expressions *laughingstock, break the ice, full circle,* using *to elbow* as a verb, *Knock, knock! Who's there?* and dozens more. How is it possible that his kids were illiterate?

Well, here's the rub—that's *Hamlet,* by the way—my daughter can't play the ukulele. That's a bit embarrassing, don't you think? I've written two ukulele books, recorded five ukulele albums and filmed four ukulele DVDs, and yet my own my child can't play the ukulele.

Is her inability to play an instrument my fault? If so, where did I go wrong? Maybe I was too encouraging. (In my book *The Ukulele Entertainer* I humorously suggest getting kids interested in music by using reverse psychology. *Tip #8: Give your child something to rebel against. Make sure they see you visibly groan every time the instrument comes out of its case.*) With me, any hint of my daughter's musical interest was enough to send me hurtling out the door to buy a piano, install a drum kit and rent a trumpet. But nothing lasted. She wouldn't practise. Her desire to *play* manifested in more social rather than musical ways.

I'm a great believer in the power of play. And when I see how self-confident and wise my daughter has become, I put this down in large part to her being allowed to spend unlimited time playing with her friends: discovering worlds of imagination, instigating new ideas, squabbling, fighting and negotiating. But she didn't experience much isolation. Her friends with tighter reins on their time were often kept indoors to study and practise. They learned to play musical instruments.

One type of parenting is not necessarily better than another. Kids often let you know what they need. My daughter, I believe, has natural musical ability, but without her own inner urge to develop it, I felt and still feel there was little I could do. Especially since my parents didn't push me too hard. I taught myself harmonica at age fourteen and didn't learn a string instrument until age nineteen. In many ways I'm glad I came to music later and through my own inner urging.

If you are a parent of a musical child, remember that there are two kinds of parental pushing. Category 1 is the kind that leads to bitterness, angry recriminations, bedroom walls painted black and an everlasting hatred of authority. Category 2 is the kind that inspires joy and creates an everlasting love of music and other kinds of creative expression.

First decide which kind of parental pushing you want to do. If category 2, then I have good news: it *is* possible to engage your child's musicality. But it takes a great deal of care and thought. It involves sacrifices of time and energy you might have preferred to put into other things. That kind of parental encouragement is a talent in itself with its own set of skills, its own efforts and rewards.

Since I was not a *pushing* parent, I have only come across these techniques second-hand. But I've seen them work well. A great way to begin is to create for your child an environment where they are around other musical kids. No child wants to be the freak: the only kid carrying a euphonium to school. Category 2 parents have even relocated to a home that is near a reputable school of music and arts.

The early stages of playing music can be a bit of a grind for children. (In adolescence the rewards become self-evident as they receive adoration for their skill, travel opportunities, friendship, amorous attention and money.) But to begin with, bribery is usually involved. Bribery may sound like a dirty word, but it's shorter than typing positive reinforcement. The point is to get your child associating musical practice with good things. Kids love games, so creating some sort of a success scoreboard to chart their advancement is one way to reward their work.

Create a collection of rewards for achievements. Examples might include earning time for video game playing and similar activities you're trying to limit. And after every three practices, say, let your child choose an item from a box of treats. Just cheap things: small toys, snack bars, toothbrushes, that sort of thing. Keep the box stocked and let them choose.

Ten practices could earn them a visit to the movies, a restaurant or a park.

With creativity and love, you and your child can be a team. You can push them without becoming a tyrant. Remember what music is about. Rapping the knuckles of the undisciplined student with a yardstick is no way to nurture a love of music (in case you were thinking of doing that).

As for my daughter, I said she can't play the ukulele. Actually that's not true. When I came back from my last tour, I discovered that she had made friends with a ukulele player in her class. He has been showing her some chords and she has started playing. She loves it. At nineteen she is too old to be a child prodigy, but now I think about it, she's the exact age I was when I took my first baby steps with a stringed instrument—a banjo.

CLAWHAMMER UKULELE PART I: WHAT'S THAT ABOUT?!

My personal journey into the art of clawhammer banjo, a technique with a distinctive sound that also works on ukulele.

I ONCE TALKED A bank teller into giving me £300 sterling—at a time when my bank account was nearly empty—because I "needed" to buy a banjo. It was 1984 and I was in my second year of applied physics at Liverpool Polytechnic. My passion for banjo had been ignited by a dreadful-sounding tenor banjo that I'd dug out of my parents' attic (dreadful to others, that is—to my ear it was the music of angels), and I made the life-changing decision to blow the money I'd saved for a car on a five-string banjo instead.

At that time I was doing my industrial placement at WIRA in Leeds, England. WIRA stood for Wool Industries Research Association. If you've ever watched James Bond films where they're testing the latest spy gear, working at WIRA was a lot like that, only wool related. The laboratory hummed and snapped with machines that caused wool to pill and break. Meanwhile technicians in lab coats walked back and forth on carpet tiles all day long to test the tiles' durability. My job was to develop a laser-activated industrial yarn machine. It never worked while I was there, but I've since been told such machines are now the industry standard. (By the way, this is all I'm telling about the seamy undercover world of wool. In fact, I've already said too much. I may have to muffle you.)

The striking-looking stockroom guy at WIRA (striking because he had one blue eye and one brown) also happened to be a part-time musician. When I mentioned my desire to play banjo he said one word, "Bluegrass?" I had no idea what bluegrass was but it sounded brilliant, so the very next day, a Friday, I was downtown buying a banjo during lunch break.

I picked out a Yoshi: a Japanese copy of a Gibson Mastertone (again, no idea what that was, but it sounded cool beyond words). I also bought finger-picks and a book called *Bluegrass Banjo* by Peter Wernick. They lay on the counter as I wrote the cheque. The man took the cheque and said, "You can pick up the banjo next Wednesday."

"Whuh?" I replied. "I need it now!"

This was technically only true in the sense that, in my obsessed state, I truly believed I *needed* to start my banjo career immediately.

"I'm sorry," said the man, "but the cheque has to clear."

I ran to the National Westminster Bank to get cash. The bank teller took my cheque and walked off. He came back to tell me, "You have only twelve pounds in your account."

I was ready for this. "I know," I said, "but *I have to buy a banjo.* I've got the money but right now it's in my building society account in my hometown. On Monday I'll withdraw it and put it in my bank account."

To further strengthen my case, I added, "I promise."

He heard my plea and stared at my impassioned face a moment before saying, "I have to talk to the manager."

The teller came back to tell me, "We've called your building society to verify you have the funds. We'll give you the money, but you need to transfer the funds into your bank account as soon as possible on Monday."

I still can't believe that this transaction actually took place. Imagine a bank handing over that much cash to a youth with only his word for collateral (Britain didn't even have ID cards in those days), but at the time it seemed a perfectly reasonable outcome. I got my banjo and carried it everywhere for several years.

My unsuccessful attempts to master the ultra-fast fingerpicking style of bluegrass lasted about a year. My failure was in large part due to my *Bluegrass Banjo* book not containing the floppy record that was supposed to accompany it. I persevered, however. Every song in the book was a mass of black dots (with typically eight or nine additional notes for every melody note), but because I didn't know how the songs sounded, I gave each note equal weight. I practised this musical morass for an hour or two every night for a year. Imagine the feelings of my housemates, being treated to a daily deluge of loud and apparently random notes. Oh, the suffering I must have caused.

Then, in Liverpool's Central Library, as if ordained by fate, I opened the local free arts magazine to behold a tiny ad for five-string banjo tuition with Sara Grey, who taught the frailing and clawhammer techniques (two more irresistible names with opaque meanings). Sara Grey, I later discovered, was a professional folk performer from North Carolina, and the frailing technique came to me as easily as bluegrass had been impossible. I quickly learned my first song; I think it was "Sandy River Belle." She'd also taught this tune to Don McLean (of "American Pie" fame), who, if I remember correctly, recorded it on one of his albums. From there I soaked up a new song every week, mostly Appalachian Mountain tunes such as "Shady Grove," "Waterbound," "June Apple," "Kitchen Girl"... eventually a long list.

Sara changed my life. She gave me a student rate for the lessons, lent me her records and took me along to her live album recording. Hanging out with the musicians before the show and listening to their hilarious banter was formative in my decision to make music professionally. Within eighteen months I was earning coins playing Appalachian old-time banjo music to Brits on the streets of Exeter, Liverpool and Sheffield.

Oh, and in case you're wondering, yes, I did put £300 in the bank first thing on Monday after getting my banjo. It never crossed my mind not to do that.

CLAWHAMMER UKULELE PART 2: THE BUM-SHIK-CA STRUM

Where I attempt to describe, in my own words—and without an accompanying floppy record—how to play the clawhammer/frailing techniques on ukulele.

IT'S THE PERSISTENT drone of its repeating fifth string that makes the five-string banjo such a distinctive instrument. When you first see the fifth string—or drone string, as it's often called—you never forget it, because it's a strange little string whose tuning peg is found standing alone by the fifth fret on top of the banjo neck. Fortuitously for ukulele players tuned in my-dog-has-fleas tuning (a.k.a. re-entrant tuning), our instrument has a high-pitched fourth string that can be played just like the banjo's fifth string. This quality makes the frailing and clawhammer banjo techniques accessible for ukuleleists.

Frailing (or clawhammer) produces a unique and engaging folk sound that combines melody notes with background strums—while continually sounding the bright plink of the high string. The terms "frailing" and "clawhammer" get used interchangeably for a strumming style that creates a "Bum-Shik-Ca" or, if you like, a "Claw-ham-mer" rhythm. All the melody notes are plucked with the back of the fingernail as the hand moves downward. So, in four simple steps, here's how it's done.

STEP #1 Strike down on a string (just strike the first string for now) with the back of your index or middle fingernail. Either finger is fine. This gives you the "Bum" part of the "Bum-Shik-Ca" sound. Bring the hand up again.

STEP #2 Brush down. The curled fingers of the hand brush down the strings using the backs of the fingernails. You may brush down them all or just a couple of the strings.

STEP #3 As the hand goes down, the thumb of the strumming hand rests momentarily on the fourth string.

STEP #4 As the hand comes up, the thumb pulls away from the fourth string. (Note: This movement is not the same action as an independent thumb-plucking action. To frail smoothly and at speed, the thumb pluck has to come as a result of the upward hand movement and not from a mobile thumb.) The brush-down plus thumb-pull combine to make the "Shik-Ca" sound.

To do justice to the above instructions, you really need to hear frailing/clawhammer in action. I teach the technique on my DVD *Essential Strums for the Ukulele,* but there are also many online examples of banjo and ukulele players using this technique. The sound is bright and cheerful and requires a flexible wrist, as opposed to the more rigidly straight wrists of most guitar and bluegrass pickers. It's kind of interesting that the hand shape—thumb plus two fingers of the strumming hand—also resembles a carpenter's clawhammer.

At first when making the "Bum" sound, aim to hit the first string only: that's the one closest to the floor. Once you can hit that one consistently, try to make your "Bum" on the second string every time. Then alternate between the two. Move on to the third string, and eventually you'll be able to strike down on any string your mind wants your finger to go to.

You may notice that the clawhammer style is fairly simple to understand but difficult to do well. This is typical. It may take months for your basic strum to sound rhythmic and musical. You'll need to develop the ability to hit whichever string you want with the back of your fingernail. You'll also need to maintain a steady rhythm played at a consistent volume.

OPEN TUNINGS

The wonderful interplay of melody and rhythm that marks the characteristic sound of frailing and clawhammer is made possible by having the instrument in an open tuning. Banjo players generally play in open G tuning (GDGBD). This means when they strum across the open strings they hear a G chord. Open tunings make less work for the left hand, as the fingers can play melody while doing less of the full-on chord work. The disadvantage to open tunings is that they make playing in other keys more difficult. Win some, lose some.

TUNING A GCEA UKULELE TO OPEN C

You can play your ukulele in an open tuning that sounds like the banjo's open G by tuning it to open C. This higher tuning is because of the relatively higher pitch of the ukulele compared to the banjo. Tune to open C by lowering the first string from A to G so your uke is now GCEG. (D-tuned ukes similarly retune to open D by tuning to ADF#A.)

Many other open (or modal) tunings are also available. These are not unlike what the Hawaiians use for "slack key" playing. If open tunings are not for you, then it is quite okay to use the clawhammer technique on your regularly tuned ukulele.

Next I'll describe some right- and left-hand techniques that add to the richness of the clawhammer and melodic clawhammer sounds. Keep listening to players you like and absorb the sound they make. Clawhammer is not for everyone. It's challenging to do well but can be rewarding if that's the sound you want. Practise with the goal of making your sound into one that *you* would want to hear.

CLAWHAMMER UKULELE PART 3: TWO NOTES FOR THE PRICE OF ONE

Playing slides, hammer-ons and pull-offs to bring more melody notes into the strum.

MELODY NOTES ONLY happen on the "Bum," that is, when the fingernail strikes down, since the brush-down plus thumb-pull (a.k.a. "Shik-Ca") is essentially background sound. You can imagine how playing a melody note only on every "Bum" would lead to rather predictable tunes, which is why fingering techniques for the fretting hand have been developed that help us to get more than one note from every "Bum." They are called slides, hammer-ons and pull-offs.

Slides are played by sliding your finger either up or down the string immediately after it has been played. Let's say your finger is on the third fret of the first string. Immediately after striking the string, slide the fretting finger from the third up to the fifth fret. Do so in the same time you normally play a single beat, so that your "Shik-Ca" comes in its usual place. You can reverse this by *sliding down* from the fifth to the third fret.

Hammer-ons are played by "hammering" your finger onto the string as soon as it has been played. For example, play the open first string, then immediately hammer down on that string. Do so with the middle finger of the left hand in the space between second and third frets. Instead of "Bum-Shik-Ca" the sound is now more like "Bum-Ba-Shik-Ca." (Or, if you're into rhythms named after woodworking tools—*à la* claw-ham-mer—might I suggest: Black-n-Dec-ker.)

Pull-offs are the reverse of hammer-ons. But it's not enough to simply lift your finger from the string after it has been played. You have to give the sound some extra help by plucking the string with your fretting finger as it comes off the string. For example, play the first string while pressing between the second and third frets. Then immediately pull the fretting finger off the string in a downward motion so as to pluck the string with the finger-end. This also gives you a Bum-ba-Shik-Ca / Black-n-Decker rhythm.

Practise these strumming techniques individually and then alternate between hammer-ons and pull-offs while throwing in a slide here and there. Make sure to sustain the clawhammer feel throughout without changing speed.

MAKE MORE MELODY BY DOUBLE THUMBING

Double thumbing is a way of adding ever more melody notes to your clawhammer playing. Here's how to do it (try doing this on a C chord to begin with):

1. Strike down on the first string with the back of your fingernail.
2. Pluck down on the second string with your *right thumb.*
3. Strike down on the first string as before.
4. Thumb the fourth string.

Double thumbing is played to the same Bum-Ba-Shik-Ca rhythm, like hammer-ons and pull-offs. What I just described is the most basic form. Experiment by double thumbing on different strings (first and third, second and third, etc.). At first you'll play mostly clawhammer rhythm, with double thumbing added in only occasionally. But as you develop your technique, you can use double thumbing to bring more and more melody notes into your playing.

Melodic clawhammer style has fewer brush-down strums and more individual note picking. Develop this style further and you'll be able to pick melodies using the thumb and the back of a single fingernail, with barely any strumming. The resulting sound is more comparable to multiple notes of bluegrass than to regular banjo strumming.

There are countless arrangements of (mostly folk) tunes for melodic clawhammer style. The sound is quite similar to bluegrass, though with fewer notes. Every note is the result of striking strings with either the fingernail or thumb, as they work together in the double thumbing technique. It's neat to be able to play melodic lines in this way, but it's a big step from basic frailing to playing complex melodies and requires dedication.

If you're a fan of my music, then you may be aware that I play very little clawhammer ukulele. You may wonder, therefore—given my earlier banjo expertise—why that is. And, quite frankly, I've wondered that too. I think my reluctance comes about because when I switched from banjo to ukulele (around 1990), it opened up a whole new repertoire for me. As I learned the songs of the 1920s, '30s and '40s, I was perfectly happy to let the folk songs slide away as my musical interest progressed. Nowadays if I use clawhammer I typically do so to add musical flavour, and the technique is rarely called upon for an entire song. Also my body got so trained to play clawhammer on a big banjo that I find it curiously claustrophobic to play those songs on a little ukulele. But I cannot deny that I had some happy years playing clawhammer and, if that's your thing, I hope you do too.

TREMOLO AND VIBRATO: WHAT'S THE DIFF?

The wobbling, warbling, pulsing sounds of tremolo and vibrato, when used artfully, add enormous nuance and feeling.

IN MY EXPERIENCE most ukulele entertainers use vibrato completely unconsciously in their singing and barely at all in their ukulele playing. Tremolo, on the other hand (and it is played on the other hand, as a matter of fact), is used predictably on ukulele but is barely understood as a vocal technique. Let's start with definitions.

VIBRATO DEFINED

Vibrato is a rapid alternating of pitch. When you hear vibration in a singer's voice, it is usually because they are quickly sliding between two notes that are slightly out of tune with one another. Often both notes are also out of tune with the song but, being just above and below the correct note, the combined effect makes it sound correctly tuned. This is a useful covering strategy for those who have trouble singing on pitch. The effect can come from nervousness, be deliberate or can develop as an unconscious habit over time.

Vibrato on ukulele is achieved by repeatedly stretching and slackening the string(s) at the fingerboard.

TREMOLO DEFINED

Tremolo is a rapid alternating of volume. Vocal tremolo is made by producing a single sustained note and quickly changing the airflow using the stomach muscles. On ukulele this change in volume is created by the quick repeated playing of a string (or several strings) using the strumming hand. (A second definition of tremolo is the rapid alternate playing of two separate notes, most frequently heard on keyboards and hammered instruments such as the marimba.)

TREMOLO AND VIBRATO FROM YOUR UKULELE

Tremolo is a way of sustaining notes. Violins, tubas and electric guitars have the advantage that each note can last many seconds, whereas the sound of a plucked ukulele string dies away almost as soon as it's been sounded. It's not really possible to make acoustic ukulele music with notes lasting more than two or three seconds, so a way around this is to do what mandolin players have done for centuries: a string is played rapidly (usually with a pick) to create a long, pulsating note. The strength and rapidity of the pulsations can be varied to create profound musical nuances.

Multi-string tremolo (strumming quickly up and down several ukulele strings) is the most commonly used song ending heard in all ukuleledom. It's not necessarily a bad thing, but permit me to suggest you take some time to work out other song endings and perhaps think about using the tremolo technique in other parts of songs. There is no ukulele law that says you have to keep one type of strum going through an entire song. Change it up a little and put in some tremolo when appropriate, perhaps in a slower section or during a high point of the lyric's story arc.

As mentioned, vibrato on ukulele is made by rapidly stretching and slackening a string after it is played. There are several different ways to achieve the effect. One is to rock your fretting finger quickly from side to side on the string. This achieves vibrato but the degree of stretching is quite small. Another way is to push the string vertically up and down. This creates a much greater degree of string bend. A third way is to push the string directly into the fretboard itself, with the finger placed behind the fret. Again this allows only a small degree of string bend.

Just as vocalists often (unknowingly) combine the effects of vibrato and tremolo, it is quite possible, although more rare, for ukulele players to do both at once, since each of the effects are provided by separate hands.

VOCAL TREMOLO AND VIBRATO

In truth it can be hard to distinguish vocal tremolo from vocal vibrato, since both techniques are often used simultaneously. But skilled singers know when to use and how to control these two techniques. For an example of vibrato and tremolo being pushed to the hilt, think of Edith Piaf. Her rapidly vibrating vocal sound was filled with an intense and urgent energy, stirring great emotion in her listeners. Widely used by French singers of that era, the sound was emulated tirelessly by everyone from stage professionals to housewives. But be sensitive that this technique, as shown by many an aspiring chanteuse, can become irritating if overworked.

Frank Sinatra preferred a cleaner and more direct sound. Hence the crooner style of singing has very little warble to it. A cappella harmony singers also work to eradicate all vibrato from their singing, since the fluctuating pitch messes with harmonies. Interestingly, tremolo, being a single pitch with changing volume, is often allowable in a cappella groups.

Listen to singers you admire, notice how they use vibrato and tremolo, and try to figure out how much of each they are using. And then listen to yourself. An onslaught of über-vibrato can be annoying, so learn to control it if you can.

Experienced singers use vibrato or tremolo to make long notes change over time. For example, hit a note without vibrato or tremolo, then add in some slow vibrato, and finally speed up the fluctuation as the note nears its end. Singer k.d. lang describes this technique in terms of her homeland on the Canadian prairies. She holds the note flat and even (like the Canadian grasslands) for a long stretch, and then towards the end the vibrations rise up like the Rocky Mountains. I don't believe for a moment that her singing style developed from the terrain in which she grew up. Rather she has acquired the technical skills and applies them with taste and care.

Sustaining a long note (in tune) without vibrato or tremolo is a developed skill and one that all singers should work towards. Once you can do it, try bringing in a controlled vibrato (or tremolo) and slowly change its rate of fluctuation. It's not easy. But it's good to be aware of the sound you are making and to caress and mould your natural vibrato into something that comes across as sensitive and discreet.

So what is the payoff for all this work? There really isn't much, because when vibrato and tremolo are used well they go unnoticed by most listeners; the audience will simply have enjoyed your music. Isn't that reward enough?

Two

SING BETTER AND WRITE SONGS

HOW TO BUILD A MUSICAL SHED

Knowing your melody is very important. So are good neigbours. Especially the ones who can teach you a thing or two.

NEIGHBOURS CAN BE handy things. Take my neighbour Doug. Whereas I am a musical performer who likes to do a bit of amateur carpentry from time to time, Doug is a carpenter who enjoys singing in amateur musical theatre. We get along great. He is of a similar mind to me in that he's always quick to make light of the serious, take seriously the ridiculous, and burst into song with the merest encouragement.

He's fairly new to the neighbourhood, so I invited him over one afternoon to try some of my U Brew cider and tour him around my shed. As I explained to Doug, the unnecessarily large and half-built shed I inherited has been a source of perplexity for some years now. Its basic construction was solid but the details left a lot to be desired, like the four windows that were really big old glass sliding doors, residing in bent and scratched aluminum door frames with handles still attached. The door itself was non-existent: just a formidable nine foot by ten foot hole where there really ought to be something. But in the last four years I've never been able to decide what. Doug had an answer.

Two days later he came by clutching a flapping sheet of graph paper with a drawing of my shed, but which now included a pair of oversize French windows. It looked terrific. The French windows, essentially large glass doors with wooden frames, would be constructed by Doug using the glass from two of the sliding doors. After making approving noises for several minutes, I told Doug that I would get him to make the doors while the rest of the work—filling in the old windows and so on—I would do myself. Inevitably we gradually tired of conversing about carpentry and got onto the subject of singing. Doug asked, "Does Kathryn sing?"

Over the years, Kathryn, my wife, has made several attempts at singing but never got anywhere. As I explained to Doug, along with some eye rolling on my part, "She doesn't seem to understand that in order to be able to sing, you first have to know both words and melody to at least one song."

Doug laughed. And so, warming to my theme, I began a lecture. "You know, without that bit of key knowledge it's kind of difficult to sing. Indeed, a cappella harmony groups will often delay harmonizing while spending several weeks with all members singing just the melody of a new song together. This has at least two benefits: One is that every singer becomes intimately acquainted with the rhythm and the phrasing of the words, so when they do split off into harmony they will be tightly synchronized. The second is that harmonizers get to know exactly what they are all harmonizing with.

"Most people don't realize this, but melody singers and harmony singers are doing very different jobs. Melody singers sing the part that everyone recognizes as the tune. The only reference they have to tell them what the next note will be is the last note they sang. The job of the harmonizer, however, is to be in harmony with the melody—whether or not that melody note is right or wrong. The sparkly bits of harmony have to hang from the tune like stars in the firmament. So, if the melody voice strays to a slightly flatter or sharper key, the harmony voices don't stick rigidly to what they know to be correct; instead they behave like good harmonizers and adjust—no matter how wrong it might be—to whatever the melody voice is singing."

As a ukulele player, you may think that the playing of an instrument gives the singer a reference point to ensure accurate tuning. But I would argue otherwise. If you are using your ukulele to locate the tuning of your next note, this probably means you don't truly know the melody.

Not being *au courant* with the melody can have pretty dire consequences. If part of your attention is always on listening to the uke for your next note, then there's a far greater chance of that note being flatter than either you or your audience would like. In addition, the declining confidence from not knowing your melody leads to further wrong notes and subsequently begets forgotten lyrics, as it dawns on you that this performance is not going as well as planned. So, know your melody!

Over the next few days I removed one of the remaining windows from its aluminum door frame and endeavoured—without any knowledge in or previous curiosity about window construction—to make a window frame. I took my time, measured everything carefully, and banged the nails in hard once I knew for absolute certainty I was correct.

Of course, I botched it. My idea of what I thought a window frame was supposed to look like was in several ways quite at odds with what proper carpenters think.

Doug was kind. "It'll be okay," he said. "You can paint stars on it and people won't notice."

I wasn't going to be doing stars. But at the thought of undoing my mistake and pulling all those nails out, I moaned, saying, "I'm so used to being inventive and doing things my own way, I really thought I could do this."

Doug replied, "No one ever regretted taking the time to make sure something was done well." And, as an afterthought, he added. "Always learn the melody first."

That's a low blow, don't you think? I mean, it's one thing to invite a person to correct their misdeeds with daubs of asteroids and comets. But to take someone's story and then use it in metaphor against them; well, I mean to say, it's downright unneighbourly!

THE UKULELE AS A SONGWRITING TOOL

A look at what makes the ukulele a perfect instrument for writing songs.

THE UKULELE HAS long been used by songwriters for composing songs. Mel Tormé, famous as a great singer, was also a highly skilled songwriter. As well as "The Christmas Song (Chestnuts Roasting on an Open Fire)" he also wrote about 250 other songs. He did not play ukulele in his performances but he, and many other talented singer-songwriters, have used the ukulele as their go-to accompaniment for writing songs.

My views on the art of song creation changed dramatically when I started on ukulele. Prior to that I'd played five-string banjo in the frailing and clawhammer styles, and I felt myself destined to be a folk singer-songwriter. I even recorded an album (only ever available on cassette tape) called *Rocket Ralph Backstep.* I thought my songs were pretty dang hot. Indeed, I have heard worse, but it was the acquisition of a ukulele that changed everything for me.

The ukulele led me directly to the songs of the 1920s, '30s and '40s. That period has been called the Tin Pan Alley era in reference to the din of composers who plinked at pianos within the offices of music publishers concentrated along a short section of New York's Broadway. The sound as heard from the street was likened to pans being bashed together. It was a fertile breeding ground for songs at a time when fortunes could be made from selling music. The motivation of monetary gain was what caused the art of songwriting to be developed to populist high art and refined down to its very essence.

When I discovered those songs, I gave up on my own songwriting for many years. My feeling was that with so many sublime songs already in existence, what earthly business did I have adding to the already monstrous pile of mediocre material? So I made it my business to quit writing songs and instead to study the greats: Irving Berlin, Dorothy Fields, Cole Porter, Walter Donaldson, Gus Kahn, Harold Arlen, Hoagy Carmichael and so many others. Mine was a homemade university course—with a student body of one—designed to study the ways that chords, melody and words can touch the human soul.

Eventually I began writing songs again and discovered that I'd learned two things: (1) I was now a far greater critic of my own work than before. Where once I'd been satisfied with a first or second draft, I now continued honing songs endlessly before I felt they were ready for performance; and

(2) the ukulele is a great tool for songwriting. And I'm not alone in thinking this; as I said, many songwriters have discovered the superiority of the simple ukulele over more traditional and complex instruments, such as piano and guitar, for bringing their songs to life. Here are some additional tips from my songwriting education.

KEEP IT WITH YOU AND TAKE IT EASY

Songwriting requires us to snatch those fragile gossamer wings of inspiration as they flutter through the ethereal world of our consciousness, inviting us to notice and memorialize them forever. And it's so much easier to keep a ukulele at hand to capture those moments than it is to always have a piano or guitar at the ready. Plus, the diminutive physicality of the instrument, with those gentle nylon strings, is much easier on the body and fingers if you're working away on a song for a long time.

NOODLING IS GOOD

Noodling, or *messing about on your instrument*, is the act of musical mindlessness. It is the aural equivalent of doodling and is frowned upon by musicians as an irritant. But take heed! Noodling has oft been the genesis of songwriting gold. Those little noodles can be the key to discovering the seeds of a melody or chord sequence from which new compositions grow. Once again, it's the portability of the uke that enables us to noodle more often and in more places—say, in the kitchen, in the car or, dare I suggest, in bed—than those bigger instruments.

KEEP IT SIMPLE

Ukuleles also make for wonderful musical economy in the sense that, despite their small size, all the notes and chords you need are right at your fingertips. There are indeed chords that contain more than four notes, but they are not necessary for most songs. The four strings of a uke are perfectly ample.

AVOID POLISHING A TURD

Thanks to all kinds of production techniques, a composition with dreary lyrics, uninteresting chord changes and a forgettable melody can be made to sound pretty impressive when endowed with a strong beat, a dozen violins and a ripping horn section. Play that same song on a ukulele, however, with all those bells and whistles removed, and you can hear it for what it is—which is not much. Hence the ukulele is a great test for the quality of a song. It strips it down to its bare essentials, displaying both its greatest and poorest qualities. This is valuable information for a songwriter who is honing her latest work. So before you enter the studio and try to make something beautiful out of something that is intrinsically rotten, play that song on a ukulele. If you pay close attention, your little uke will clearly tell you whether your raw creation is ready for the bigger world.

TEN TIPS TO WRITE BETTER SONGS

Ideas to help you achieve masterful melody manipulation and wonderful word weaving.

WHEN A FAN of my albums *Love* and *Laughter* wrote to tell me that he appreciates my "clever songwriting and wordplay that reward close and repeated listenings," he endeared himself to me in two ways: first, he proved there are still some people who engage in active listening, and second, he showed me there are those who pay close attention to the art of songwriting.

There's no magic recipe book for manufacturing hits. And it's a good thing too, for great songs usually contain an element of the unexpected: some surprise to delight our ears. How to invent those sweet surprises? Well, that's the tough part. There is no map for finding serendipity. We can only hope to be in the right place at the right time and have the foresight to recognize it when it visits. But despite music's ability to make our spirits soar, songwriting is still a down-to-earth craft, and many elements of that craft can be learned and mastered. Let's look at what makes a well-crafted song and how to go about writing one.

TIP #1 ***Grab the ephemeral.*** You can create space for new song ideas by removing obstructions to your daydreams. Everyone has their own way to do this; find yours. Lie on the floor in an empty room, travel, meet people, sit up all night, go for a walk, wake up early. Whatever works for you is what you need to do. Make sure you have some means to record song ideas and have the sense of purpose to grab voice recorder or pen no matter how inconvenient the circumstance. Be conscious and aware of your own sense of creation.

TIP #2 ***Write lots, edit later.*** Leonard Cohen and Bob Dylan are highly regarded as wordsmiths par excellence. But their work styles differed in that Dylan would talk about completing songs in a short period of time (hours or days), whereas Cohen said he sometimes spent years perfecting his lyrics. However, one thing they had in common was that both shared the technique of writing more verses than would appear in their final work. Both knew better than to accept the first ideas to come along as being the final product. Only by pushing further will you accumulate the material from which you can choose the very best.

TIP #3 ***Aim to write melody before lyrics.*** The overriding philosophy amongst Tin Pan Alley songwriters was "Melody first, then lyrics," and they held to this maxim for good reason. It's important to remember that song lyrics are not poetry. They die or fly depending on the melodic wings with which they are bestowed. Music has a way of bypassing our intellect, and this fact makes it far more likely that perfect words will be inspired by a melody rather than the other way around. When a melody is grafted onto a lyric, the tune tends to be uninspired and intellectually driven. But as with any general rule, there are notable exceptions: Dorothy Fields and

Jerome Kern wrote their 1937 Oscar-winning song "The Way You Look Tonight" with lyrics first. And classically trained Elton John formed his greatest songs by putting tunes to Bernie Taupin's lyrics.

TIP #4 ***Try chords first.*** A favourite way I have of writing songs is to look for a chord progression and rhythmic feel that pleases me. By getting those things right, you have a better chance of laying a decent melody and lyrics on top. By working this way I often find that words and melody originate almost together, back and forth, inspiring one another in a leapfrogging sort of way.

TIP #5 ***Let the song tell you what it needs.*** Do learn from your predecessors, but know when to go with your instincts. Don't add extra verses or a solo because you think that's what you're supposed to do. A song can be shorter or longer than what you consider "normal" and may contain other elements deemed eccentric. Remember that the "hook" of a song (that unique quirk that makes the song stand out in a good way) is always different from the run-of-the-mill. Allow it to be surprising by doing what the song demands.

TIP #6 ***Write from a place of emotion.*** A good place to start is to write your song from a place of strong feeling (although it's not a prerequisite, as volumes of wonderful music have come out of contradictory emotional or neutral states). I find that writing from your gut has a way of clarifying the thought processes. However, it is quite possible, even likely, that the message the audience hears may have nothing to do with the original intent of the writing. When Chris Difford of the 1970s band Squeeze wrote "Tempted [by the Fruit of Another]," he was writing about his discovery that their bass player had been approached by another band. Listening to the song, you just assume it's his girlfriend who has been tempted to leave. Howard Kaylan, of the 1960s band The Turtles, wrote "Elenore" with deliberately flawed lyrics as a way to get back at his record company's demands for "another 'Happy Together,' " their previous hit. However, such inept lines as "You got a thing about you" and "You're my pride and joy et cetera" (who uses "et cetera" in a song?) came across as heartfelt expressions of teenage exuberance and the record buyers loved it.

Another example is one of my own songs, "Movie Stars, High Rollers and Big Shakers," which began life as an emotional rant about an aborted Las Vegas performance. I was happy with the chords and tune, but the lyrics made the song unsuitable for family audiences. On the suggestion of another songwriter I rewrote the lyrics to be about a failed Las Vegas marriage, and the song came together.

TIP #7 ***Simplicity is king.*** Remember when you first felt joy? Or love, curiosity, sadness, playfulness, jealousy, laughter and rage? Probably not, since those moments happened early in your childhood. What was the state of your vocabulary at that time? I'm betting it wasn't full of words like "verbosity," "erudition" and "loquaciousness." Our fundamental emotions are connected to simple ideas expressed through short, childish words. Laugh, fun, like, love, blue, bird, sky, happy and now tend to work better than their counterparts: hilarity, enjoyment, comparable, endearment, azure, feathered creature, firmament, contented and presently. The same goes for your melodies: beautiful and uncomplicated tunes will connect best with most listeners (although sadly, with a century of copyrighted songs already behind us, the best tunes have pretty much all been taken).

TIP #8 ***Declutter your song.*** It's distressing to cull those beloved verses that once meant so much and may have taken hours to complete. But if they no longer serve the song, then you have to let them go. You'll know you've done the right thing if you feel lighter and better off for having eliminated the excess. It's like decluttering your home of junk. Songwriting doesn't reward pack rats and hoarders. Know specifically what your song is about, and make every lyric serve the main message of the song. Watch for unnecessary repetition. If there are lines in your song being sung more than once, ask yourself to what purpose. Repetition, depending on how it is used, can either be a powerful way to hammer a message home or it can be a powerful way to induce boredom.

TIP #9 ***Don't quit till it's done and know when to quit.*** The most common mistake new songwriters make is in thinking their song is complete when there is still much work to do. I'm not the only one to have grimaced while listening to some expensively produced drivel from a singer-songwriter who has gone ahead and recorded a song that is still in its first draft. When you think your song is finished, keep playing it to yourself. Be hyper-alert for any line or verse that gives you a small but uncomfortable feeling of something not quite right. Be ultra-vigilant for melodic lines that sound like they could have come from one of a thousand songs. Get super-critical of parts that niggle. Ruthlessly hunt down awkward phrases and make whatever changes necessary. But leave the good stuff alone! Many music and lyric choices don't make intellectual sense; they just feel right. Develop the wisdom to know the moment when there's nothing left to add or cut: that's when your song is finished.

TIP #10 ***Creativity works like a muscle.*** Make a habit of creativity and exercise it often. Know that much of what you create, especially in the beginning, will probably never be worthy of performance, but that's okay. It's more important that you do *something*. Make songs that take the listener on a journey. Figure out how chords and melodies create tension and release, and craft your song to include those climactic moments. The best way to learn is by actively listening to other people's songs; memorize, dissect and analyze them, and thereby become a more effective self-critic.

DARE TO BE SHARP!

Are you singing in tune? Really listen to yourself and try these tricks to avoid torturing your audience.

I ONCE PERFORMED IN a vaudeville show. These happen periodically when yet another misguided show producer decides the public is again thirsty for ten-minute-long variety acts. A big drawback with this idea (other than the mind-blowingly obvious: why would anyone pay to see such a thing when YouTube and similar video sites are essentially free?) is the inconsistency of local live acts. Vaudeville's essence was that each act had something that was unique and special. But all too often the special quality of some acts is the sheer awfulness of performance.

The show I'm talking about had charismatic singer who sang "Summertime," from *Porgy and Bess*. Her loud and resonant voice packed heartfelt emotion into every syllable. Her voice swooped down, rose up and vibrated the walls on every crescendo. It would have been a showstopper were it not for the fact that she sang consistently and jaw-droppingly flat. The worst of it was that nobody told her. After the show, overhearing her friends and fellow vaudevillians complimenting her on her "amazing" singing, I was finally moved to exclaim, "What, are you all deaf?"

Having got their attention, I faced the woman and in front of the whole cast said, "You, lady, sing flat. A performing dentist's drill would have extracted fewer winces than your effort tonight. If you're going to sing for paying customers, it needs to be in tune. And you, my dear, have some major work to do in that department."

Actually, no. I didn't say any of that. Show people are notoriously vulnerable, and no one wants to be the one to deflate their bouncy castle of optimism and hope. So I'll say it to you instead. "You sing out of tune and you need to do something about it."

No matter who you are, I'm probably not far off the mark with that statement; it's just a question of degree. A note-perfect singer is a rare being.

We all need to work on our tuning. It's important because how in-tune you are pretty much decides whether your voice is on the side of beautiful to behold or painful to bear. And here's the thing: no amount of ukulele practice will improve your singing. They are completely separate skills.

Start listening to your own voice. Listen honestly and without judgment. Hear the sound you're actually making and not what you want to believe is there.

CHALLENGE YOURSELF

Here's a game you can play to see how well you stay in tune over the course of a song. Play and sing something you know well. At the end of the song, hold the last sung note and find that same note on the ukulele fretboard. Now sing the song again. Use the ukulele to help you get started on the right note, but then stop strumming and sing the rest of the song unaccompanied. When you hit the final note of the song, find it on the fretboard and compare it to the final note from before. Is it higher or lower in pitch than before?

My guess is that, unless you have a well-developed sense of pitch, your final note will be flatter (i.e., lower in pitch) than the first time. Keep playing this game and see if you get closer to ending on the correct note (which is almost always the key that the song is in).

If you're having trouble even finding your last note on the fretboard, then that's an issue. But don't give up hope. Ear tuning—that is, hearing if one note is higher or lower than another—gets better with practice. I used to be awful at this skill and still have bad moments. If you feel utterly hopeless, get someone more adept to help you.

MAINTAIN THE TONAL CENTRE

How do you maintain the correct key without a musical instrument to keep you in tune? The answer is the mental trick of hearing the key note in your head and then singing the song without the mental key note changing over the course of the song. This is called maintaining the tonal centre. It's an odd skill in that I'm not really aware of when I'm doing it, but I always know when it breaks down. Spend time overcoming whatever it is that takes you out of the tonal centre.

Being able to maintain the tonal centre for a whole song is a huge step, but it doesn't mean that every note you sing within the song is in tune. It's highly probable that within the song there are still several out-of-tune notes. You need to locate and correct these.

KNOW THE NOTE INTERVALS

So why do we sing out of tune? Poor vocal technique is often a culprit. If you're not singing with strong vocal support, then you're probably tending to sing flat. The other reason is not knowing note intervals. The *Porgy and Bess* lady had no problem with vocal support but she clearly had no sense of what the exact note intervals were. In "Summertime" the first note is on the *summ* syllable, the next note is on the *er* syllable, and the word "time" is back on the same note as *summ*. It's quite a big jump down in pitch and then back up again to where you started. And the audience knows the tune. So it's pretty obvious when the *time* ends up drastically different than *summ*. You have to hear note intervals in your head to be able to sing them. In other words, get to know every note of the melody and how each note relates to those before and after.

MORE TUNING GAMES

Tune your ukulele, play a note and sing it back, either to a friend or into an electronic tuner. Are you right on the note, or are you too high (sharp) or too low (flat)? Most people are flat. If so, train yourself to sing a notch higher than you usually do. *Dare to be sharp*—and you might just hit the right note.

When melodies flow up or down in steps, singers tend to make the downward steps too large and the upward steps too small. Correct this by singing downward melodies in slightly smaller steps and upward melody lines in slightly larger steps than feels natural.

Certain vowels often come out flat. The "Aaah" vowel is notorious for sounding flatter to the listener than to the singer. Seek these out and push them up a little. *Summ-er-time,* for example, has aaah vowels in both *summ* and *time*. Even *er* has some *aaah* in there.

You may be getting the idea that I want you to sing sharp. That's not the case. In fact, chronic sharpness is as bad as chronic flatulence, I'm sorry, I mean flatness. But by correcting your flat spots with some nice bright sharpness, you have the potential to lift your music out of the dentist's chair and into the realm of the angels.

CATCH THE WAVE AND SING

When someone sings well, they make the process seem effortless and natural. But how can we achieve that ability?

UNLESS YOU HAPPEN to fall into the sparsely populated category of pure ukulele instrumentalists, singing well is a vital part of being a ukulele entertainer. I often have to remind new performers that the voice is the star, and the uke, no matter how skilfully strummed, plays the role of backup band.

There is a lot going on when someone sings well. And just as a champion surfer makes riding the peak of a wave seem easy and graceful, getting your voice to float effortlessly upon a column of regulated airflow can be equally natural and relaxed.

Unfortunately, however, many self-taught singers use vocal techniques that don't support their voices. The result is poor-quality singing and, if continued, eventual vocal damage. I know this because I used to be one of those singers. I've had to work hard to make my voice deliver itself in a natural way. And it was done through a process far more laborious than some people, in their well-meaning ignorance, describe as a "gift."

My voice suffered in the past. Poor vocal technique meant that I'd get hoarse if I sang too much. I admired people with big voices. They could fill their lungs and sing and shout for hours without hurting themselves. Babies, I noted, were especially talented in this regard. If I should have chosen to bawl and scream like that for more than a moment, it would have done me irreparable harm, yet newborns could keep it up for hours. But no matter how I tried to project a big sound, it always came out sounding somewhat strained.

This little fact did not stop me from performing in semi-professional shows and amateur musicals, until I actually damaged my voice to the point of needing an operation. I had a nodule snipped off my vocal folds, and the recovery process led me to learn from several singing teachers and to join a barbershop chorus. Over time I learned to reconnect my voice to my airflow—something we all did naturally as babies—so that I could eventually sing with power and ease.

One of my teachers, Reid Campbell of Nova Scotia, described a process of *catching the wave* where he likened singing to surfing. I don't surf, but the analogy of catching a wave at just the right moment was so good that he showed me for the first time what true singing felt like. I'll describe it to you and perhaps it will help you too.

STEP #1 ***Lie down on the floor.*** If you need to raise your head, use a cushion or a book under your head to bring it an inch or two off the floor. Close your eyes. Take some deep breaths and sigh them out. Relax. Notice where your body is touching the floor and imagine all those points being in those same relative positions when you stand and sing. The straightness of the spine and the alignment of the vocal mechanism is the reason many people sing better when they are lying down. (There's an episode of *The Simpsons* where Homer Simpson becomes a great opera singer—but only when he's lying on his back!)

STEP #2 ***Keep your chest expanded.*** Place your fingertips on your chest and inhale deeply. Feel the ribs expand. Do it again. Now this time when you breathe out, don't let your chest drop. Keep it big, like an opera singer. Use the muscles in your chest to keep the chest big and barrel-like. Continue to breathe in and out while keeping your chest expanded. You may notice that keeping the chest expanded in this position means that your breathing has to come from the diaphragm (the muscle below your lungs) and other abdominal muscles.

STEP #3 ***Make a vocal impulse.*** While continuing to breathe, gently place your hands on your belly. Feel it rise and sink as the air goes in and out of your barrel-like chest. While this is going on, imagine that a friend has just given you some news. It's neither good news nor bad news, so you react in a non-committal sort of way. You have no comment to make. All you can offer is a *Huh* sound. When you say *Huh*, your belly moves impulsively inwards. Catch yourself by surprise. Imagine the news being given and feel the subsequent inward jerk of your belly as you go *Huh*. Do it again and again.

STEP #4 ***Catch the wave.*** That simple *Huh* may seem rather inconsequential right now, but this is analogous to the moment that surfers call *catching the wave*. The wave is your airflow, and your voice rides that wave in direct connection to your belly. Now all you need to do is lengthen the *Huh* and you'll be singing.

STEP #5 ***Ride the wave.*** This time do three *Huhs* and on the fourth time let the sound continue for as long as you can: *Huh Huh Huh Haaaaaaah*. If I have described this well, you are now making a nice long vocal sound that connects directly to the muscles producing the breath control way down in the belly.

STEP #6 ***Practise every day.*** Get used to doing this. Quite soon you can replace the *Huh Haaaahs* with vowel sounds: *Mah, May, My, Mow, Moo,* etc. Try changing the pitch of the notes: sing higher and then go low. Eventually go on to sing song lyrics. And when you stand up to sing, remember to keep the chest expanded, the neck long, the chin tucked in slightly, and everything else nice and relaxed.

Connecting the voice to the flow of air is the very basis of singing. If you don't have that working for you, then nothing else is going to sound all that great. Of course, there is a lot more to learn in becoming a good singer, but if you feel confident in the above then you're off to a great start; and you didn't even get wet—if you did it correctly, that is!

SING LIKE A RUBBER UKULELE

If you feel your voice sounds thin and insubstantial, then these vocal techniques are just for you.

FEW PEOPLE HAVE an accurate mental picture of exactly where their voice hails from. Common knowledge tells us that our throat contains a voice box, or larynx, within which the vocal cords reside. Such language gives an imperfect picture of the vocal mechanism. For one thing, voice box sounds altogether far too rectangular and rigid for what you actually see when you look in there. And the so-called vocal cords don't so much resemble cords as they do a folded piece of rubber tubing. Hence the more correct term: *vocal folds.*

The vocal folds are connected to the sides of the air passage by muscles that we unconsciously control to make sounds. Other uses of the larynx include closing off the air passage to stop food being inhaled and reflexively coughing in order to eject foreign particles. The physical size of the vocal folds determines to a large extent how high or low your voice can go. Men have weightier folds and therefore sing deeper; women's lighter folds enable them to sing higher. But other than that, the vocal folds are limited in what they can do for you as a singer. They control pitch and volume, but that's pretty much it.

Your larynx and vocal folds don't affect the quality of your voice. In fact, the quality of your sound is mostly all in your head. And I mean that literally. If you've heard the terms "head voice" and "chest voice," forget them; they are very misleading. Your vocal resonance is not affected by your chest. Anyone who has heard Toronto jazz singer Alex Pangman can attest that her beautiful vocal sound remained essentially unchanged even after a double lung transplant. The term "head voice" is often used to describe falsetto singing. Falsetto, or the technique of singing in a very high range, is actually achieved by a pinching together of the vocal folds. Thus the vocal folds and chest play only minor roles in how your voice sounds, and it's the air space inside your head and throat that really determines vocal quality.

Every ukulele and guitar has a resonating chamber, giving the instrument its distinct sound. This is why ukuleles generally tend to sound *plinky* and guitars more *boomy*. Human beings, however, have the interesting advantage of being able to change the size and shape of the resonant cavity inside their head. The degree to which we can vary our vocal resonance is akin to having a rubbery ukulele that can be stretched to guitar size and shrunk back again at will. Developing the ability to do this, however, takes practice and playfulness. (By the way, all practice should be playful. If it isn't, ask yourself why not.)

Few complain that their voice is too resonant. The only exception I know was a childhood friend of mine whose playground voice carried so well that teachers always picked him out for unwanted attention. The fact is that most people's voices are thinner and reedier than they would wish. The need for most of us is to create more resonance. So how do we do that? Simple: create more space inside your head.

- ***Start with the mouth.*** Going in through the point of entry we first notice inflexible material: teeth, gums, hard palate, and so forth. We can't do much there. But the tongue is soft, so play around with ways of flattening it, bringing it back, making it wide and low, and so on. The back of the mouth is flexible too. Try enlarging both the throat and the softer palate at the rear of the mouth. One trick is to open your mouth wide and react as if someone has thrown a baby hot potato into the back of your throat. Imagine the sharp intake of breath and notice how the back of the throat and soft palate reflexively expand. Alternatively, imagine swallowing a tennis ball. See if you can hold the expansion and try singing with a larger vocal cavity. We're so used to how our own voices feel and sound that these techniques will seem odd and unnatural at first, but work at it.

  Touch the outside of your throat approximately where the larynx is. While singing "Aaaah," change the expansion in your mouth and throat. You should feel the larynx drop down as the cavity and resonance increase, and physically rise again as the resonance, and space in your mouth, decrease.
- ***Relax the jaw muscles.*** Gently massage the point where your jaw meets your head. Imagine chewing on a rubber hockey puck, and feel how the distance between the back teeth must expand to accommodate such a thing.
- ***Get rid of mucus.*** Once you've established expansion in your mouth and upper throat, the only cavities left are within your sinuses. Obviously you'll get more resonance with clear sinuses. To this end singers prepare for performances by causing their faces to vibrate with all sorts of weird buzzing sounds. This is followed by an encore of nose-blowing, all done in an effort to clear mucus. Famous singers don't advertise it much in their autobiographies, but believe me, it's a common practice.

  If your sinuses seem eternally plugged, the problem could be dietary. Cow dairy and wheat are the usual culprits in this regard. Both of these modern products have been hybridized to the point where our bodies have trouble digesting them. Look into replacements (goat dairy and low-gluten grains, for example) and see what works for you. Nasal irrigation with a saltwater solution and regular aerobic exercise can also help to clear the airways. Being in good physical shape is great for any occupation, but especially for singing.

- ***Play with the concept of expanding your range of vocal qualities.*** Discover in yourself the characteristics of different types of singers. Mimic them. As well as improving the overall quality of your voice, these techniques also offer you a tool with which to inject meaning and emotion into your voice. And you never get to the end of this process, so get used to it!

YOUR MICROPHONES AND YOU

Guidelines for choosing the appropriate amplification devices and their various accoutrements.

THERE ARE IMPORTANT choices to be made when purchasing microphones to plug into your PA. But before we discuss microphones, I feel it is important to first say a few words about another vital component of your entertainment equipment.

THE MICROPHONE STAND

Tall, thin, silent and elegant: the presence of a microphone on a stand adds focus and gravitas to a performance. Think of the singer who walks out and stands at the microphone. The inanimate mic stand is a pedestal for an object that makes humans sound like gods. It draws the audience focus almost as much as a bright spotlight can. For sheer charismatic appeal, it has few peers. A friend of mine, singer-guitarist Josh Minsky, equates the presence of a microphone stand to having a second performer onstage with you. The microphone and its accompanying stand are seldom pondered, but they're as vital to the performer's stage presence as the costume and the smile. I urge you to consider this phenomenon if you ever consider getting a headset microphone. Such a microphone may be suitable for dancers, clowns, evangelists and anyone else who needs to jump around and wave their arms about, but unless you absolutely need to be fully mobile, I'd suggest staying with the traditional set-up.

The stand may have a weighted base or be the tripod style with folding legs. I prefer the latter as it tends to be lighter and easier to store. And get yourself a microphone boom too—a rod attached near the top holding your microphone out and away from your stand—thus creating room for your ukulele and strumming arm. If you're also using an *instrument microphone,* then you don't need to buy another stand. Instead you can get a clamp that attaches to your existing stand. The clamp supports a second boom, which holds your instrument microphone.

And, while we're at it, let's mention microphone cables. Keep yours tidy. Unless you're going to be walking around onstage, coil the cables along and around your stand and have the excess cable wound into a nice coil on the floor (not trailing all over the stage like a tapeworm looking for its long-lost home). When you coil up your cables to put them away at the end of the gig, there's a special way to do that so they don't get all knotted. (There are videos to show you how, or get a stage technician to reveal the secret.) And here's a useful bit of information: If everything is plugged in and switched on correctly and you still get no sound from your microphone, it's almost always the cable that is to blame. A cable can work fine one day, be left overnight and then, for no apparent reason, be faulty the very next day. So before you buy a new mic, rewire your amp or start yelling at someone—check the mic cable.

THE VOCAL MICROPHONE

The industry standard for vocal microphones is the Shure SM58. It's the cardioid, dynamic (ice cream cone-shaped) microphone you always see performers using. There are better-sounding microphones in the world, but this is a reliable and robust microphone that rarely lets you down. For optimal sound quality you need to sing close to the microphone, say, about

3 or 4 inches. In other words, your mouth needs to maintain a distance from the microphone equivalent to the width of your fist. Your body can gyrate all it wants, but your head needs to stay still if you don't want the sound to get louder and quieter.

THE CONDENSER MICROPHONE

With this microphone the performer, or performers, can stand a few feet behind the microphone. If you use a condenser microphone to pick up the total sound from your voice *and* the ukulele, then positioning is very important. The microphone needs to be placed in such a way that the voice and ukulele volumes are in balance. This microphone is more forgiving with movement than the dynamic microphone, and the sound quality can be excellent. Sometimes whole bands will stand around a single microphone to play (country and bluegrass bands especially). But there are some limitations. Feedback can be a problem with these microphones, especially in noisy group situations. They also usually require a power supply such as a battery or 48-volt phantom power (usually supplied by the amplifier; see page 127). Condenser microphones also pick up more external sound than you expect, so watch your mouth when you turn away to say things that you think the audience can't hear. Before buying a condenser microphone, make sure it's what you need and that your amp can supply the phantom power if necessary.

THE INSTRUMENT MICROPHONE

If you want to plug your instrument directly into an amplifier, then your ukulele needs to have a pickup either built into it or stuck onto it. For information about ukulele pickups, read my earlier book, *The Ukulele Entertainer*.

Ukulele pickups prevent feedback, but you generally get the best sound when using an external microphone. Once again the Shure company can claim the most widely used instrument microphone of all. The Shure SM57, invented by Shure engineer Ernie Seeler, is a microphone you can use onstage or in the studio. It's reliable and won't let you down. In fact, it's been used to amplify speeches by every president since its introduction in 1965. Mr. Seeler expected his microphone to be used for classical orchestras. He despised rock music, for which, ironically, his microphone has been most used. There is no word on what he thought of ukuleles.

When buying sound equipment: Remember that being louder does not equate to sounding better. Seek equipment that retains as much of your natural acoustic sound as possible.

MEMORY AND PERFORMANCE

This chapter is all about, er, no, don't tell me... ooh, I know this one, no, don't tell me... Damn! It's gone.

I REALLY WISH I could give you one easy method to help you memorize songs, but I can't. The human mind is a mystery even to those who study it in detail. Our minds all work differently from one another. The way I learn a song may be entirely at odds with how you do it. As if that weren't enough, the stress of performance can change everything. It's common to find ourselves unable to remember even the first word of a song that we often sang flawlessly at home. These things considered, here are some ideas to help you commit songs to memory.

ALLOW YOURSELF PLENTY OF TIME

Through trial and error I've found that I learn songs slowly but well. If I have to perform a song without music in front of me, I make sure to be working on it at least three weeks beforehand. Although I've been known to memorize a song quickly, sometimes in just a few hours, playing it generally culminates in missed chords, absent words and even whole forgotten sections of the song. Having a longer lead time does two things for me. First, it allows the song to become a part of my being; I want the song to sit comfortably in my psyche so I hardly need to think what word or line is coming next. Second, it helps enormously with confidence. It's stressful to sing a song onstage that was committed to memory only the day before. I'm much calmer if I've already been singing a song for some time.

A PHOTOGRAPHIC MEMORY DOESN'T ALWAYS HELP

Although it would be nice to instantly commit lyrics to memory, I would not want to do so at the expense of performance quality. One player I know has a photographic memory. He can quickly store any number of songs in his memory bank. He's also a very musical person and has no problem with stage fright. Sounds ideal, yes? Yet his performances are technically well executed but woefully uninspiring. He doesn't make eye contact with listeners. His eyes are looking up in the air and moving from side to side. It's as if he sees the song lyrics inscribed above the heads of the audience, who, for the most part, sit bored and unmoved. Enjoy the process of learning great songs: research them, mine their hidden depths to seek new meanings in the words. Develop a process that works for you. Figure out how long it takes you to fully commit a song to memory. Collect techniques that help you to learn. Try these:

- ***Work on the song often*** and for short amounts of time.
- ***Get away from using the paper*** as soon as you can.
- ***Sing the song to yourself when not playing ukulele.*** Leave your music devices at home next time you go for a walk or bicycle ride. Use every opportunity to sing your song over and over to yourself.
- ***Let your subconscious do the work.*** Practise the song last thing at night before going to sleep and again first thing the next morning.
- ***Rehearse creatively.*** Play the song for an imaginary live audience, again and again.

PREPARE FOR THE BIG NIGHT

Eventually you'll know how long it takes *you* to get a song ready for that nerve-wracking initial presentation. As with first impressions, you get only one chance to sing a song in public for the first time. Sometimes the result is a disaster. But (and I always find this effect interesting) if you've done your work well, then it is possible that the first time out with a new song could be the best performance of it you'll ever give. I'm not completely sure how this happens. It seems that the product of the work, plus heightened focus and the raw awareness of being onstage, often contributes to a performance that a crowd finds completely captivating. It's like a high-wire act. You don't even need to tell the audience that you're unveiling the new song. Their animal instincts sense the fact that you are stepping into thin air and could fall at any moment. It's a thrill for them and a powerful moment for you. And oh, what a relief it is to get to the other side and step onto solid ground once more!

BEWARE OF THE SECOND TIME

The most dangerous performance is not the first one, it's the second one. Don't be lulled into a warm feeling of security that the worst is over. I tend to make more mistakes on the second outing of a song than on the first. So I urge you to prepare for the second performance as if the first one had not even happened.

ALL IS CALM, ALL IS WELL

Are you an emotional singer? Here are some thoughts about that.

THE STATE OF calm is a rare commodity. The Internet and personal communication devices have set our lives a-wobble on the quicksands of ever-increasing change. The purity of our air and water is in jeopardy as oil, forestry and mining companies enter a technological renaissance, fracking, hacking and drilling in places unreachable just a few years ago but now boring our world to new levels of extraction. And, if that weren't enough, robots and automation are taking over everything—delivering us not the promised utopia where robots do all the work and we get to be on permanent vacation, but an Orwellian reality where the only winners are the owners of the robots. And that's just the normal day-to-day stuff.

On top of these concerns get layered all the little daily issues: kids, parents, work, school, cars, transit, lost keys, broken appliances and the endless need to communicate with everyone through half a dozen media. And that's if things are going well. We live on a knife edge. But our emotions truly get tested when something devastating or unexpected enters our experience to further jar whatever tentative equilibrium we've managed to muster.

In November 2013 I got a call from a fan phoning long-distance from the United Kingdom. In a deep, rich Southern England voice he apologized for phoning but felt the need to tell me his story. His name was Giles. As he began his tale he paused to inhale deeply, saying to himself, "Come on now, Giles, hold it together."

He'd just been to call on an elderly neighbour: someone who rarely left the house. As he approached the house Giles saw that no lights were on. With mounting worry Giles knocked on the door. No answer. He called through the letterbox and ran around peering through windows. By now he was sure that something terrible had happened to his neighbour; his panic was rising as he imagined various tragic scenarios. Then he remembered there was a family that the elderly fellow would visit very occasionally. Giles ran home and phoned the family. And that's where the man was, enjoying a pleasant evening.

But Giles's heart was still pounding. He told me, "I needed something to calm me down, Ralph, so I reached for my iPod—I have well over a thousand songs on there, all bought from iTunes. Don't tell my wife, she'd have a fit if she knew how much money I've spent on music. And I said to myself, what do I need to calm me right now? And you have to understand, Ralph," he said, "my iPod has songs by so many greats: the Beatles, Pink Floyd, Doris Day, Rogers & Hammerstein, Puccini, Burt Bacharach, Joe Walsh, Jo Stafford, George Harrison, the Drifters, the Mills Brothers, the Bee Gees, Bob Seger, Madonna, Crosby, Stills, Nash & Young, I could go on and on naming the artists whose music is in my collection. But out of all of them I picked you. In my state of shock, Ralph Shaw was the only name that sprang to my mind. And listening to your music calmed me right down."

About a week after that phone call from Giles, I called my parents. My mum told me how my dad had been talking to an old work colleague on the phone when his wife, Valerie, asked if she could talk to my mum. My dad handed the phone over and Valerie—whose daily life is an ongoing struggle thanks to the effects of Parkinson's disease—said to my mum, "I just wanted to tell you how much I listen to Ralph's CDs. I put them on often because they help to calm me down."

I wondered if this was simply a coincidence or whether it was more than that—perhaps some special quality of my music. So, out of curiosity, I contacted Giles to ask if he could put his finger on what it was about my music that he felt had calmed him. He answered, "It's because you've got a beautiful voice and the songs you choose are so unthreatening and non-aggressive—just peaceful, restful and beautifully non-2013. The ukulele is my favourite instrument—but I adore the way you play and sing. *Gentle*, that's the word."

A common error made by singers is to believe that the emotion a singer feels will somehow be transmitted to the heart of each audience member and become their emotional experience too. But it's not true. In a singer's effort to emote, they block their own ability to be a conduit for the song. The job of a singer, especially in the learning stages, is to clear themselves of emotion and to fully attend to the business of singing well. If that is done, then each audience member will receive their own personal experience rather than being observers of the performer's inner drama. The singer's chief responsibility lies in devotional servitude to the song.

Great singers are also great actors in that they develop the ability to play the part of the character singing the song. This is especially noticeable in musical theatre, but to a more subtle degree is also apparent in other musical styles. Actor-singers learn to portray outward emotions while at the same time committing fully to the sound production. When done well, both acting and singing come across as uncomplicated and natural, but are truly much more difficult to do than the general public realize. As such, they are two of the most misunderstood of all arts.

I was surprised to learn that my music can work as a soothing balm for the emotions—for two people at least. I've never recorded or performed with an intention to extract a particular emotion from listeners, but the idea of it pleases me. So if you listen to my music for relaxation, then all I can say is: You Keep Calm and I Will Carry On!

CHRISTMAS—WHY DO WE DO IT?

"The only good thing ever to come out of religion was the music."—George Carlin

---

As I GET older I find I become less and less interested in the season of goodwill and all its trappings. I no longer race around looking for gifts. Two years ago, when my daughter was eighteen, she told my wife and me, "No gifts." She said she didn't need any more junk or useless possessions and had no use for unwanted gifts. This release from the burden of gift buying came as a happy relief. We gave her a little cash instead—*that* was still welcome. Of course, I still look forward to receiving a gift or two myself, since I'm not quite so spiritually developed as she is.

Christmas is the best time of year. And it's the worst time of year, depending whom you ask. It's a time when memories of either magic or tragic childhood Christmases are triggered once again. Emotions run to the surface and spill over, causing us to wallow blindly in well-worn feelings. My own Christmas memories tend to be of the cozy warm glow type, but I've met plenty of people who don't feel the same way. One friend told me his mother passed away just before Christmas when he was eleven years old, and the sights and sounds of Christmas reignite his deep loss on an annual basis. Which does not exactly fit the dictionary definition of the word "merry." Another friend said his father was a happy, likeable man all year round but exploded in rage and misery every Christmas Day. Good grief.

You have to think, what is the point of it all? Is all this Christmas malarkey really necessary? Why do we do it to ourselves? Why do we bother? Every year as Christmas approaches I ask myself these same questions, and every year I am answered in the same way. No matter how grumpy I am in the run-up to Yuletide, my mindset gets completely turned around for the same reason: the singing. This is the one time of year when a whole lot of people of all ages know a whole lot of the same songs and have a terrific time singing them together. It really is that simple. The joyful benefits of singing together are not to be underestimated. It's a powerful and friendly force.

I am so lucky to be an entertainer in December. I feel so good after my gigs that I can barely contain my joy. Kids, adults and old folk dress up, sometimes in silly Santa hats, red noses and antlers, and sing and laugh and dance around. They smile and sing and jingle those daft little bells. It's wonderful to be the instigator of their hilarity. I go home and regale my family with stories of what I experienced. I think I get more of a festive feeling from Christmas-season gigs than I do during Christmas itself—which is pretty low-key in comparison.

So my message to you this and every year is, no matter how you feel about the seasonal shenanigans, get yourself out to a place where you can belt out some songs with a bunch of friendly folks. I mean it—it's the best cure for the wintertime blues.

THE ART OF THE SINGALONG

Thoughts on what was once a part of everyone's life and has now all but disappeared: the good old-fashioned singalong.

THE LAST GREAT group of singers was the World War II generation. They kept the rickety pub pianos vibrating with song and laughter well into the 1980s. But since the pubs were renovated, and those cranky old tack pianos cast out along with the battered cigarette machines and charred lampshades, we turn our heads to discover that those old songsters are also mostly gone. Some of those veteran singers survive, but the ones who do are now into their nineties and harder to find gathering for a singsong at happy hour. As each one passes away, so do more memories of that generation's great moments. It was an age when every event was marked with music.

Sure, there are still a few places where one can stand around the piano with like-minded veterans of song—perhaps to croon hits by the likes of Vera Lynn, Bing Crosby or Al Jolson—but they are rare now. One example is Vancouver's Billy Bishop Royal Canadian Legion hall. Their regulars still drink pints and sing songs every Friday until midnight, when they all link arms for the final medley. Their sadly departed pianist, Bea Blackwell, played an almost unbroken line of weekly singalongs and annual Remembrance Days for many decades.

One obstacle to the modern singalong is that even amongst those who can or would like to sing, there is no common repertoire. Let's say we had an opportunity to get together and sing—what then? How would we choose the songs? I can imagine much vying over whether to sing rock 'n' roll, rhythm and blues, ragtime, rockabilly, reggae or rap.

The demise of the family piano is also partly to blame for the decline in singalongs. Once it was the family's entertainment system, but now the piano has been taken over by that huge, black, rectangular void: big-screen TV.

Thoughts of all this came very strongly to me recently when I was booked to visit the family home of a prospective client. Her brother had mentioned me to her. She told me, "My father is going to be ninety years old and he loves to sing, and I can't think of a better birthday gift than a family singalong. I hear that you lead singalongs and even do house calls."

This was a misunderstanding and I could see how she had come to this conclusion. Yes, I have been known to entertain in people's homes and yes, I do lead a monthly ukulele get-together—essentially a singalong for strummers. However, a family singalong with people I'd never met was a new idea for me. But I liked the concept and went with it.

Right away I realized that with an age difference of eighty years between oldest and youngest, deciding what to sing would be the first issue to work out. My solution was to suggest to my client that she create a songbook for the occasion. I emailed her a number of song suggestions from my own repertoire. Armed with these songs, plus additions of her own, she came up with a selection of ditties that would hopefully cover the tastes of everyone at the party. The book she made was spiral bound and had a picture of her dad on the front. She sent a copy for me to work with.

Not long after, I was in their family home in the pre-dinner hour standing on a fireplace rug and leading a boisterous family singalong. It struck me what a rare privilege this was. The ukulele had taken the place of a piano, but the unique feeling that comes from a group of voices singing happily together still remained. Mostly in unison and occasionally in harmony we crooned, amongst other hits, "Blue Moon," "For Me and My Gal," "With a Little Help from My Friends," "Rubber Duckie" and a song with some particular meaning for me, "Edelweiss."

As we sang of the alpine flower that greets us every morning and whose snow-white petals we urge to blossom and grow forever, I found myself thinking back to past singalongs in my life, to the many singers I've known, some no longer around, but whom I suddenly remembered clearly. Along with an almost painful ache of nostalgia came a barely remembered sense of tender belonging, a nearly forgotten feeling of warm togetherness, that I'm sure used to be more commonplace. My memory suddenly felt sharper and richer thanks to the words and melodies of the songsmiths, whose powers included the ability to conjure up long-neglected senses and recollections.

Every November 11—Remembrance Day—I entertain during a rousing singalong at the Billy Bishop Legion. It's a time when I'm annually reminded of the phrase "Lest we forget." And as we remember the lost, the brave and the good, I suggest we also spare a thought for the humble singalong, whose very presence in our lives gives us something to live for.

HOW TO LEAD AN AWESOME SINGALONG

With the blossoming of the ukulele, the potential for group singing has become almost limitless. Here are ten tips for great singalongs.

To simply sing with others is a basic human need as essential to our social lives as eating and drinking. But although they were once as natural as the afternoon nap, singalongs don't happen by themselves. They require a special person: someone to organize and motivate a group of wary screen gazers and transform them from habitually passive observers into shining pillars of song. If you think you might be one such person, here are some hints to help you get it right.

1. ATTRACT WILLING PEOPLE

Ideally folks should know ahead of time that they are going to be singing. That way they can bow out gracefully if they want to. If your crowd contains too many arm-folded non-participants, then you'll be fighting an uphill battle.

2. BE A LEADER

Being a leader means several things. It's up to you to put across the idea that singing in a group is a completely natural and acceptable thing to do. Be confident and enthusiastic. Be more outrageous and silly than you normally are. If others see you letting go, perhaps they'll be more willing to unshackle their fettered spirits and free their voices. A good leader is there to serve the group by keeping things fun and flowing. This means creating a plan but also having the flexibility to stray from the plan when inspiration takes the group in unexpected directions. Avoid being over-controlling and pushy.

3. WELCOME ALL TO PARTICIPATE

In our world where everything musical is presented as something to be observed by others, the philosophy of unwatched group singing can seem a very foreign concept. In a singalong the listeners are the same people making the music, so there should be no fear of outside judgment. As a leader it is up to you to find every way you can to make the singers understand this. Whenever anyone comments that they will sing quietly because their voice is no good, firmly and kindly tell them that there are no bad voices. Nothing matters except to *do your best and have fun doing it.*

4. GET OTHERS TO LEAD

Spot the stronger singers in the group and offer them the chance to lead one song or more. This is an especially good idea if you are a better organizer than you are a song leader.

5. CHOOSE WELL-KNOWN SONGS AND STAY CLOSE TO THE ORIGINAL

Your singalong will be a very quiet one if people don't know the words or the tunes. I recommend you pick songs that are known by at least a slim majority of your fellows (say, 60 percent), and it can be helpful for cohesiveness to keep close to the arrangements of the famous recorded versions that most people know. Fancy phrasing and stylizing make it harder for others to follow. This is not a fast rule, however. It can be a lot of fun to play a song completely outside the genre in which it is usually heard. I recently led my group in a high-speed rendition of "Amazing Grace" that clipped along at breakneck pace while still somehow suiting the song.

6. KNOW YOUR MATERIAL

Practise the songs before venturing to lead them. Make sure you know the beginnings, endings and the starting note. You'll make mistakes as you go but remember the mantra: *Do your best and have fun.*

7. KILL THE VIDEO AND PHOTO

The recording of sounds and images implies that someone will eventually observe and judge our efforts. This creates tension no matter how polite the cameraperson may be. No one likes to have their image taken while eating, so why allow video and photos while singing? You're in a group but it's still private time, and just because someone owns an expensive piece of gadgetry doesn't automatically give them the right to use it. For the most part our wannabe paparazzi think they are far better at photography than they actually are. They believe that pressing a button is an art form. It isn't. Next time someone starts "taking" your picture without permission, tell them you'd prefer that they set up an easel and paint your image instead. See what kind of an artist they truly are. Seriously, though, let your group decide the culture they want. For example, they may choose to allow video and photos for one or two songs only. Do what you wish, but I would strongly advise against unlimited recording.

8. INCLUDE VARIETY

Most songs are repetitious, and singing a song the same way twice can get boring. Find ways to vary the music. For instance, get the crowd to sing sections by themselves, without you leading. Change the strumming style and the volume level. Play with the phrasing a little. Do what you can to make the same words and chords seem interesting all over again. If you have several short songs that are fun but which don't bear repetition, then just let them be short or consider making them into medleys.

9. ENCOURAGE WITHOUT COMPLIMENTS AND CRITIQUES

Offering words of encouragement like "Sing louder!" and "Oh yeah, you got it now!" loosens up voices without inflating and deflating personal egos as individual remarks can do. Conversely, pay close attention to what the group is telling you. React to their comments and gestures. They may provide inspiration that you can draw on to make the experience more spontaneous and exciting.

10. RELISH THE MOMENT

A singalong is never the same way twice. It is timeless. Compared with such a reality, the production values of even a space-age high-definition 3-D holographic camera are as empty and worthless as dry dust. It's a precious time. Be fully present and remember, because it can't be said too many times: *Do your best and have fun!*

SO YOU WANT TO MAKE A UKULELE SONGBOOK

Considerations when producing a ukulele songbook, as well as an answer to the question "Should classic songs be changed to make them easier to play?"

AS THE LEADER of a ukulele club, you want to keep everyone happy. Hey, why not? We play ukulele to be happy and we sing with others to be happy, and we want everyone to enjoy the repertoire. So we pick songs that will satisfy most of the people most of the time. It's only when you're in the position of making song decisions that you discover a myriad of ways to make the wrong choices.

FAVOUR CHESTNUTS OVER MODERN SONGS

The songs should be recognizable by about 60 percent of your participants. This percentage has not been arrived at by any scientific means. In fact, I made it up. But the point is this: If your club songbook contains obscure songs, no matter how great those songs are, they will simply not get played. They become a waste of paper, time and effort. Including songs in the hope they'll magically become popular by their inclusion in a songbook rarely works.

Modern songs (songs from the late 1980s onwards) are similarly problematic because they haven't stood the test of time. Just because a song was a big hit amongst the record-buying public is no guarantee of its immortality. Almost everyone recognizes "Blue Moon," "Blue Skies" and "Blue Christmas," but big hits from more recent acts like, say, Jack Johnson, Jewel or Carly Rae Jepsen, although adored by certain (large) pockets of people, are not well enough known to make them singable for the general public. The Internet has resulted in fragmented audiences. Before the 1990s, thanks to TV and radio, we were connected by the same songs and TV shows. That just isn't the case anymore.

Another curious phenomenon is how prevailing songwriting styles have changed in the past twenty years. In earlier decades songwriters took care to come up with strong melodies and then fit the words exactly to those melodies. Such songs have straightforward phrasing suitable for group singing. But at some point, and I'm not sure when or why (perhaps it was the combined influences of Bob Dylan and then rap), a more recitative style of popular songwriting emerged. Words no longer matched the tunes. Songs became rambling, albeit poetic, accounts of thoughts, emotions and events. So unless you are intimately familiar with how the original artist sang the song, it is near impossible from a page of lyrics to guess where to place the words. Therefore consider modern songs carefully before putting them in your book. In many cases only time will sort out future classics that have lasting singalongability.

PICK THE BEST-KNOWN ARRANGEMENT

Bear in mind that great play-along songs are usually associated with one particular version. For example, many people know the song "Me and Bobby McGee," but it's the Janis Joplin version that they think of, rather than the one by its songwriter Kris Kristofferson. Most people will want to sing it in the style of Janis rather than Kris. Transcribe such multi-artist songs with that in mind, as it can inform your arrangement choices (such as where to put instrumentals, which verses to include, which lines get repeated, and so on).

CHANGE THE KEY AS NEED BE

Once you've picked your song, the next dilemma is what key to put it in. The obvious choice is to place it in the key of its most famous recording. This has the advantage that you can play along with it. The problem comes when the key is almost unplayable for most ukers. I'm thinking of keys like E-flat, E, B, F-sharp, C-sharp and G-sharp. All these keys have people laying their GCEA-tuned ukes down as they quit keeping up with the "weird" chords.

When changing the key of a song, here are some things to consider:

- ***Who will be singing?*** If your group is mostly women, they will prefer a key that is different to what your men would choose. For example, I generally find if I'm comfortable singing "Happy Birthday" in the key of C, most women would rather it be in the key of F (and vice versa for other songs).
- ***Who leads the singing?*** Pity the poor song leader who has to stand up front and squeak out a song that's not in his key because the key was picked for women's voices. It's a process of give-and-take. Try to be somewhat fair with your song key choices. If you have songs in keys that are

sometimes unsuitable for either the leader or the group, then that's okay. This might even encourage someone else to get up and lead a song or two.

SHOULD SONGS BE ADAPTED FROM THEIR ORIGINAL VERSION?

Once you've got your ideal song and found the perfect key to play it in, you may then discover, as you scan the sheet music, that there are oodles of chords that sound great, but their difficulty makes the song daunting. Should you simplify or not? Everyone has their own view about changing songs. Such views range from those who diligently seek out the published sheet music and don't change a note, to those who copy and paste the first set of lyrics and chords they find posted on the Internet at 1 a.m. by some unknown imbiber of who-knows-what. It's worth noting that even a composition that seems hokey and obvious was often painstakingly crafted by its composer to be that way.

Ukulele songbooks and the Internet abound with songs written down in ways that are different from the songwriter's intentions. But many people who use these versions for group playing are not aware of this fact. Musicians have always learned songs by ear, without ever seeing written versions. In the past these personalized and usually incorrect versions of songs would only be viewed within the transcriber's immediate circle of musical friends. Now, thanks to the Internet, songs with misheard lyrics and bad chords can be read, copied, emailed, printed out and passed around by a people's distribution system that would have been the envy of twentieth-century music publishers.

As the person putting together a club songbook, should you make adjustments in order to make songs more playable for your people? I say yes; the benefits of changing to a singable key and easier chord changes (which hopefully still sound decent) usually outweigh the downsides.

Final note: Sometimes a song or two may need to be included for "political" reasons. By these I'm thinking of occasions when someone who does a lot of work for the uke club sends you some songs that they've lovingly transcribed. They may not be ideal songbook candidates but hey, if some of the songs aren't complete duds, it may be better to include them rather than lose the help and friendship of a loyal and happy ukulele comrade.

Three

PERFECT YOUR PERFORMANCE

SMILE, DAMMIT, SMILE!

Here is the first lesson for performers. Learn to smile!
Along with reasons why and tips to try.

ALTHOUGH IT PAINS me to admit it, I have finally accepted that smiling is smart. My early life near Barnsley in Yorkshire is possibly what led me to believe that anything worth doing was worth doing dourly. In 1970s Barnsley, smiles were generally saved for special occasions and not wasted on frivolities like good jokes, acts of kindness or major celebrations. Because of the culture in which I grew up, I still get more delicious mirth from a hilarious zinger delivered deadpan than from a joke told by a grinning raconteur.

Among primates the baring of teeth demonstrates a readiness for violence. In some Asian cultures, the smile is a sign of embarrassment or confusion. Other cultures reserve their smiles for friends and family. They wouldn't think to smile at strangers. Whereas an American may state that Russians don't smile enough, your average Russian will be quick to respond that Americans smile too much and in the wrong places.

From a ukulele entertainer's point of view, I have to grudgingly acknowledge that it's those over-smiling Americans who have the right idea. Smiling has many advantages. For one, it makes people more attractive to others. And get this: Economics professor Daniel Hamermesh (author of *Beauty Pays*) has demonstrated that ugly people earn less than attractive ones, are less likely to obtain bank loans and, if they are running for office, get fewer votes than those with above-average looks.

It has also been shown that people who smile receive greater trust and more help from others. Apparently your smile even helps others to remember your name more successfully. People in service and hospitality work are trained to smile. How big would your restaurant tip be if the maitre d' looked like a rainy day, the bar staff were miserable and the servers looked like their underwear was on back to front? Not very big, unless you happen to be Russian, in which case you'd probably be having the time of your life.

For some activities, like playing ukulele, a smile should be a given. After all, who wouldn't rate ukulele strumming as the happiest occupation ever invented? Ukulele players should feature highly in the category of people most likely to be constantly smiling. Sadly, this is not always the case.

Picking, strumming and singing is great fun when you can do it. But becoming skilled requires hours upon hours of focused concentration. With minds intent on wrapping fingers around an F-sharp-minor-7 chord, many people unknowingly train their faces to become quite gargoyle-like. Harpo Marx used an extreme case of this condition to create a comedic face that he named a *Gookie.* Gookie was a real person who rolled cigars in a tobacconist's window, oblivious of the fact that his neglected face was being carefully studied by the young Harpo Marx.

We know the saying "Practice makes perfect." But many players apparently hold onto the belief that being onstage will somehow magically improve their playing. Others are certain that their live performance is never as good as when they play at home. The truth is that our public performances are actually very similar to what we do when we play alone. Unfortunately, this is also true for the expression we wear while playing. I have seen many otherwise worthy performances be quite undermined by the player's tortured facial contortions.

As well as making you look more appealing, the right kind of smile can improve your singing. Smiling brightens the quality and expression of your voice. A slight lift of the cheeks plus aliveness in the eyes brings more sound to the front of the face—which is what you want. To see how this works, make a relaxed, neutral face and let your jaw hang. Sing the following words on one note, "We are playing now." Repeat the phrase a few times. Now, while keeping your voice the same, lift the corners of your mouth into a smile and sing the words again. Listen for changes in tone. Is it darker and muddier or brighter and clearer? Probably the latter. Repeat this exercise a few times. Listen carefully to the quality of your vocal sound.

In addition, when you practise, consciously relax your face and smile while your fingers strive to attain their desired degree of dexterity. As the playing gets trickier, smile more! Your performances will benefit immeasurably if your audience perceives that you take delight in attempting trickier passages. Avoid showing grief, worry, tension and other unhappy emotions that your listeners are hoping to be lifted away from.

Watch the faces of your favourite players and singers. Decide how you want to appear to others when you are in the limelight, and keep that intention whenever you play. Twisting your face to resemble Quasimodo's less comely cousin won't improve your music.

Remember: *Practice makes permanent—so be careful what you practise!*

FIND YOUR PASSION

With so much going on in our lives, it can seem pointless to even consider what our one passion might be. But there's a payoff.

I COMPLAINED TO A friend of mine recently. She's a singer named Kristie. I griped that my life has become too diverse, and I muttered that my activities have increased to the point where they are not so enjoyable anymore. Extra pressures include paperwork and endless online communication. But they also come from taking on new projects without letting old ones go. The result, I grumbled, is that I'm juggling more objects and it's becoming less fun.

I felt mean-spirited even complaining. To display a lack of gratitude for opportunities in life seems churlish when you think that 80 percent of the world's population is forced to exist in grinding poverty. But instead of chastising my selfishness, Kristie took me in a surprising direction. She asked, "What is your passion?"

"Erm, why?" I replied. "What's that got to do with anything?"

She said, "If you know your passion, then you can devote more time and energy to that and less to the other things."

I was stunned. This was new thinking for me.

Some things were easy to cross off my passion list. They included taxes, household chores and anything involving a computer or phone (basically life's unavoidable duties). Much harder to choose from were my various work-related roles: making music, giving live performances, teaching ukulele workshops, singing, creating songs, recording and writing. All these things I take pleasure and pride in. If I had to drop all but one of them, which would I keep? This spurred me on to a new round of griping. "I can't possibly! It's too hypothetical! How can I choose just one?" and so on.

With further urging, I narrowed down my top passion contenders to two choices. Kristie then asked me to imagine placing one of these in each of two corners of the room. As I closed my eyes, she reminded me to visualize the choices I had made and the parts of the room where they resided.

Kristie said, "Do you feel a pull towards one of the corners?"

Yes, I did. The attraction to one corner was unmistakable, and slightly overwhelming. Moments before this, my mind had been a confused swirl over what to do. Now my direction was clear. Apparently this was my passion. The other trivialities in my life paled in comparison and I felt a surge of deep feeling—an abiding sense that this experience was profound and true. It was actually enough to stop me grumbling for several minutes.

Many players take up the ukulele with some idea that it will lead them to their passion. Which they believe must be to perform onstage. But I disagree with this thinking. When I travel to ukulele clubs, I meet a wide cross-section of people who all happen to play ukulele. But look more closely and you'll see that the instrument is actually a conduit to many possible passions. The players come together to make music, but their natural roles soon become evident.

- ***Some are leaders,*** expressing themselves by forging a vision for the group.
- ***Some are carers,*** scanning the group looking for those in need of assistance and coming to their aid.
- ***Others are teachers,*** striving to develop their own understanding in order to pass on the knowledge to others.
- ***Some are communicators,*** developing the threads of interconnection that bind everyone together and helping to disseminate information.
- ***Some are stage entertainers,*** shining in order that we may connect with our own spirits.
- ***Some are social entertainers,*** never going near the stage but always ready to share a song or a story that will crack you up.
- ***Some are hosts,*** offering their homes and time to accommodate visiting entertainers from far away. (I have often been humbled by the kindness of strangers who host me and go out of their way to make my tours possible.)

If you don't know what your passion is, perhaps this can help: Figure out what you enjoy doing most of all. It has to be something that you feel strongly about. It should be nearly as vital to you as food, air and water—something that you'll always want to do no matter where life takes you.

If your answer is unclear, then sit in a quiet room and place your two most fulfilling activities in each of the far corners. Close your eyes and notice if there is a pull of attraction towards one part of the room. You may experience this as a sense of peace or another feeling that draws you. If this works but seems incomplete, it could be that you need to define your passion in more detail. Try using the technique more than once to refine your choice.

Knowing your passion helps to focus your energies and decision making. Do newly presented choices further your life's purpose, or are they mere sidelines and distractions? Cut out the things that no longer serve you. Although it's good for us to be diverse beings (author and waterbed inventor Robert Heinlein said, "Specialization is for insects"), at some point enough is enough.

Figuring out what you *don't* want is important. And imagine the joy you'll get in doing what you love in the place where you want to be. It's certainly nothing to grumble about.

PLAY AND HAVE FUN!

Where I offer some important, yet playful, suggestions to help you put on a show that your audiences will enjoy.

ONCE A MONTH I run the Vancouver Ukulele Circle. It's a roomful of 100 to 150 people who come along with ukuleles and pack the St. James Hall in Vancouver. They come for the enjoyment of playing music with like-minded friends. But it's obvious from their faces, and the laughter that comes out of those faces, that they also get very entertained. While at the ukulele circle their hearts get lifted, problems get forgotten and smiles get broader. You might ask who or what is responsible for this phenomenon? Well, and I say this with all humility, some of it is due to me!

When I head off to run my ukulele club, I leave home with the desire, aim and commitment to put on a great show. It's no different from every other gig I do. If you could do some sort of a clever brain scan, just as my fellow ukers and I start to play, you would notice that my mind is fully on the job of making every moment count towards entertaining my fellow strummers.

People seem to enjoy the variety. The off-the-cuff comments, the humorous asides, my improvised singing, my hot (I think) dance moves and the way I pick on individuals—in a good-natured way, of course—all add up to an evening where folks don't really know what is going to happen next and anything is possible. If I had to sum up what I do with just one word, I'd call it *playing*.

Although we are used to saying that we *play* music and *play* the ukulele, the lightness and easiness of the word gets forgotten somewhere during the practice stage; so, by the time we actually get to perform, this thing we do has become a serious business indeed. So serious, in fact, that the dread of performing can lead to paralyzing stage fright. For most of us though, the seriousness of playing music in front of others is a somewhat staid ordeal. You're so busy trying to "get it right" and "not screw up" that there is no time for the extra fun stuff. Yet that fun stuff is the element of your performance that makes it extra special.

Whenever I leave the house to go to a gig, the last words I hear from my wife Kathryn are "Have fun!" It has become something of a ritual for us. There is always a moment, just as I step into the car, that I take a mental pause to contemplate Kathryn's words and consider their importance. When people see me perform, they do indeed want my show to be of a satisfyingly high musical standard. But deep down they just want to be entertained. It's always been this way, since the beginning of humanity.

Before Shakespeare's time actors were known as *players*. I saw Ricky Gervais interviewed on David Letterman's talk show, just before Gervais was to host the Golden Globe acting awards for the third time. He was asked to justify his sharp mockery of the actors attending the awards ceremony. Letterman wondered if Gervais was perhaps being a little too cruel. Gervais replied saying, "Give me a break, they're not wounded soldiers. We're talking about people who pretend to be other people for a living. Of course I'm going to make fun of that."

People love Gervais's irreverence. And the ratings for the Golden Globes went up every year that he hosted them. But what does it mean when we say that musicians and actors are *players?* And how do we improve our spirit of playfulness? Well, if we want to be better players, I suggest we learn from the experts: *kids*. If you ever get a chance, try to eavesdrop on some children who are in the middle of free play. Listen to the ease with which ideas flow. You were a child once. Cast your mind back to a time when you had the sort of easy facility to create a mental playground with your friends. In your imaginings any space could become a cave, a palace, a hospital or a bus.

Once, when we were about six years old, during school recess my friends and I were playing at being knights in armour. One of our number, Richard Pratt, had an air of authority about him. We honestly believed that he knew everything. I tired of being a knight and called to Richard to ask, "Were there dinosaurs in those days?" Richard thoughtfully considered my question for a moment and answered, "Yes."

With glee I became a tyrannosaurus and attacked my armoured foes by breathing fire on them. That's what play is all about, and this sort of thinking is what we need to cultivate and cherish. We need to be like Richard Pratt and say yes to the silly, the abstract and ridiculous, and make it seem real enough that our audience will come along for the ride.

Improving our performance with playfulness, irreverence and spontaneity has the magic effect of bringing out those same traits in others. However, such playfulness shouldn't come by sacrificing the quality of the music we've worked so hard to achieve. It's important, therefore, to perform pieces that are within our skill level. Avoid performing songs that are musically over-ambitious. If you want to improve your performance, you're going to have to relax and get playful. You can only do this if you truly have confidence in your music.

And one final suggestion: Since it helps to be constantly reminded of the value of having a childlike sense of play, get your spouse, parent, kid or neighbour to yell out, "Have fun!" every time you leave for a gig. It works for me.

RIPE FOR THE PICKING: KNOWING WHEN YOU'RE READY

Some thoughts about waiting for the right moment.

RECORDING MY ALBUMS *Love* and *Laughter* required me to be at the top of my game both musically and artistically. I prepared like an athlete heading for the Olympics. Steve Dawson is a multi-award-winning producer who believes in capturing great performances in the studio;

so instead of multi-tracking every instrument, we recorded all the bed tracks in one shot (mostly myself on ukulele and voice, Steve on guitar and Rob Becker on bass). Each song had to be played near-flawlessly by each of us. Small errors were tolerated, even welcomed, like the imperfections in fine leather that prove its authenticity, but perfection was our aim.

Performing twenty-one songs with feeling but without mistakes requires great mental and physical readiness, and I wanted to be in peak condition. Here's how I prepared for recording:

- ***Attended to physical health.*** For fitness I did moderate running, yoga/stretching, meditation and cycling. I quit stimulants—caffeine, alcohol, sugar—to aid sleep and concentration.
- ***Guarded vocal health.*** I sang daily to strengthen my voice and drank water regularly. I also took care to avoid vocal abuse (talking in noisy environments, shouting and coughing).
- ***Prepared my instruments.*** I changed all my ukulele strings. (I recorded on five different ukes so that was twenty-six strings to change—yes, not all ukes have four strings.)
- ***Benefited from coaching.*** I took two lessons with Jennifer Scott, a talented vocal coach who answered some questions I had about singing.
- ***Prepared the songs.*** I analyzed every song to make decisions about intros, endings and where solos should go. Much of this work was changed in the studio, but you have to have things mostly figured out in order to change them.
- ***Practised.*** Mostly we didn't record to a *Click* (the metronome beat that keeps musicians exactly in time), nevertheless I practised for hours with a metronome. By the time I got in the studio, it was second nature for me to keep a part of my attention always on the other instruments.
- ***Dealt with personal matters.*** I didn't want my thoughts distracted by outstanding issues, so I answered emails, tidied my workspace and erased all concerns that could affect my concentration. I once heard of a Tai Chi

competitor who wrote his will before a championship so that thoughts of his own mortality wouldn't disturb his composure. I didn't go quite that far.

- ***Waited for the right moment.*** In my desire to record I've made several false starts. Each time when I believed I was ready to record, something prevented me from going ahead. With the benefit of hindsight, I'm now very glad I didn't force those projects into happening.

This time everything about the work felt right. From the moment Steve Dawson's name was suggested to me, I had a gut feeling that things were ready to start working out. Just like fruit is easy to pick and eat when ripe, everything in the project fell into place with a sense of inevitable readiness. You can't force this stuff to happen; either the timing is right or it's not.

Several times in my career, I've been faced with a well-meaning but overzealous parent and her self-conscious teen. The mother is saying of her son, "His music is fantastic. But no one else knows it because I can't get him to perform. We go to parties and schlep along his guitar/ukulele/accordion but he never wants to play. What do you suggest? How can I get him to perform?"

I look at the painfully embarrassed boy; his downcast eyes are fixated on his feet shuffling haphazardly below his awkward frame. For a moment I become him, I know what he's going through. I look back at Mom and I shrug my shoulders and say, "He's not ready to perform. *He*'ll know when it's time."

The boy's feet stop shuffling, but he continues to stare at his toes as Mom begins her manifesto of why he needs to "get out there" and not "hide his light under a bushel." She wants me to back her up, for my words to agree with her and somehow inject a dose of Ralph Shaw magic to transform her reclusive strummer into a denizen of the stage.

I tell her, "But he wants to get good first." The boy's eyes snap upwards at this unexpected turn of events. Mom is surprised but continues to argue the point, "Yes, but isn't it better if..., shouldn't he..., don't you think..."

I stop her. "You wouldn't want to embarrass *yourself* in public and neither does he. He'll know when he's ready. And when he is, people will watch and they'll listen and you will be very proud of him."

As the concept sinks in, mother and son turn to look at each other in a silent new understanding. I find myself supremely touched by whatever invisible force it is that gives us the inner knowing of what it means to be ready. I've been wrong about many things, but I do know there are certain feelings to be trusted. There is a time for learning, a time for waiting and preparation, and a time when fruit is ripe for the picking.

SEVEN TIPS TO MAKE IT TO THE BIG TIME

What I learned when I auditioned for Canada's Got Talent.

FIRST OF ALL let's get one thing straight: there is no "big time." The term dates back to vaudeville days, when a phenomenal performer might make it onto the Big Time Circuit. This was a tour of high-class and well-paying vaudeville theatres. Performers came from all walks of life but, if successful, were paid thousands when average working wages were measured in tens of dollars. The closest we get to a modern equivalent of big time is the television talent shows. Typical of these is the *Got Talent* franchise, such as *Britain's Got Talent* and *America's Got Talent*. I auditioned for *Canada's Got Talent* and got a first-hand view of how the TV talent game works. Here is my report on what I experienced, with the hope that you'll do better than I did.

TIP #1 ***If you don't try then you'll never know.*** I heard about *Canada's Got Talent* from my friend Geoff, who insisted I was "just the sort of thing they're looking for!" At first I dismissed the idea. From what I've seen of TV talent shows, they are overdone to the point of obnoxiousness, but I figured there could be benefits: money, fame, material for my next book and pacifying people like Geoff.

TIP #2 ***Register for your audition time as soon as you hear about the contest.*** Don't put this off until the pre-registration deadline passes. Or, like me, you'll stand in line from 8 a.m. until 6 p.m. The majority of other hopefuls were young singers (aged twenty-one and under). The females had that warbling, semi-yodel style that you hear so much of these days. They did it well. But after listening to their vocalizing all day, *distinctive* and *unique* were not labels I would hang on any of them. I learned that my style of singing is now referred to as "old school." Other acts included a large synchronized-skipping troupe, two guys balancing soccer balls, a rollerblade artiste with an arm in a sling and Canada-guy (bedecked in red tights, red hat and glasses, flippers and a Canada flag, he stood on his head to play the national anthem on a kazoo). During the whole day I never saw another ukulele player. That surprised me.

TIP #3 ***Choose the right song.*** Picking the right audition song was a puzzle wrapped up in an enigma within a pain in the arse. What would they be looking for? I figured my song should grab the judge's attention quickly. Getting attention can be achieved by being louder, faster, flashier or by being unusual, say, mellower, sweeter or from a different era. Choosing the latter tactic, I picked one of my favourite bittersweet songs by the Ink Spots, "Every Night About This Time" (recorded on my album *Table for Two*).

Even side musicians with huge repertoires don't seem to know this one, and I thought its obscure nature might be a plus. However, the warbling teenage clones suggested otherwise. "You're more likely to win with a well-known song," they all told me, nodding in agreement with each other. Following their advice I changed my audition piece to the better-known song "Brazil." I also decided that doing "Brazil" as a one-man band might give me an edge. I phoned Kathryn and asked her to bring my one-man band gear. Not hard to do since I lived nearby and was still roadside at this point.

TIP #4 ***Don't over-practise on the day.*** With hours spent waiting, you may feel like working your audition piece. While it's important to be warmed up, don't overdo it to to the point where the song gets routine and your voice gets sore. I didn't, but I watched others who did.

TIP #5 ***Have fun and keep your perspective.*** Eventually we moved indoors to the hotel lobby, then on into a large conference room. Each of us got a large number sticker to adhere to the front of our bodies, and we each signed a contract promising to attend future auditions wearing the exact same clothing and hairstyle (this news momentarily troubled the warbling clones). Waiting in the final holding area, a young guy with an earring played his original song over and over again. His guitar technique was childishly basic and his song was dreadful. I felt embarrassed for him. Yet he thought he was fantastic. It was wrong for me to judge him though. Every person there (including myself) truly believed against all odds that we had as good a chance to win as anyone else: so much self-delusion all in one place, sigh. Fortunately the real music business is not like that at all—ha-ha.

TIP #6 ***Show your best stuff and do it ASAP.*** Five of us entered the audition room, where a kind-looking gentleman sat behind a table with a video operator alongside. The kind man explained: "Give your name and town. I'll ask some questions, then you show me what you've got. Perform as if you were in front of hundreds of people. No more than ninety seconds each, please."

Considering we'd been waiting around for close to ten hours, ninety seconds may sound a bit chintzy. But I'll tell you now—it was ample. In fact thirty, or even twenty seconds would have been enough for most acts. The show is all about talent discovery. Your singular ability must be strikingly identifiable within seconds. There is no time to get acquainted with the audience. You have to be instantly brilliant. Be clear what your talent is and demonstrate its glory as soon as you can.

TIP #7 ***Try to look ordinary.*** I quickly set up my gear and the interviewer asked me what I do for a living. I wanted to tell him I had a boring day job. However, googling my name would show organizers that I'm an established independent entertainer. I reluctantly told the truth, that I've performed for many years. The unspoken implication hung in the air: "Why hadn't he heard of me?"

My decision to change my audition piece had been a mistake: the audition room made my drum sound so boomy that my singing was obscured. I also regretted wearing my suit and bowtie—too polished, perhaps? I was learning that the show has a strong "rags to riches" component: witness the hysteria that erupted when dowdy talent contestant Susan Boyle began to sing.

All in all, my years of performing couldn't get me past the first round of a national TV talent show. No surprise, really. I was up against thousands of participants from all over the country. So if you're thinking of having a crack at the modern-day big time, I suggest you hit them with your best shot, dress down and don't forget to mention your boring day job.

CHOOSING THE RIGHT MOMENT TO PLAY

Where we learn an important lesson in performance timing.

OVER THE YEARS my dad (Barrie) has occasionally mentioned that he'd someday like a surprise party. After my sister Heidi and I talked it over, we decided his eightieth birthday would be the time. So while I made arrangements to fly to the UK, my sister got on with the work of booking a location, ordering a buffet and contacting all his friends still alive and mobile enough to attend the party. (This in itself was an uncomfortable job, because as the daughter of an octogenarian, people assumed the worst when they heard her voice on the phone: "Hi, this is Heidi—but don't worry, it's not bad news!")

We managed to invite friends from most parts of his life, which is good because his life has followed an unusually varied path. He planted trees with the Forestry Commission, he walked in Queen Elizabeth's Coronation Parade as an RAF policeman, he ate penguin eggs during two years in Antarctica, was a weather scientist in Quebec's Subarctic and finally became a village schoolteacher in Yorkshire, England. But an unforeseen glitch occurred when my dad, having by now given up hope of a surprise party ever happening, took it upon himself to organize his own party. At the point where some confused friends were starting to get invites to two separate parties, Heidi had to break the news to him that festivities were already in hand. All was well. My dad had something to look forward to, but didn't know exactly what.

One of the invitees was Ed. He had been in the Boy Scouts with my dad. At some time in their late teens, Ed and Barrie went to a Burl Ives concert. It was a life-changing moment for both of them. They loved the show, and soon afterwards my dad got his first guitar. Ed, however, was more musically gifted and was soon playing rings around my dad, whose progress was much slower. Ed acquired a repertoire of Burl Ives songs and then moved on to other genres, eventually carving out something of a musical career for himself.

During the time my dad was in the Antarctic, Ed recorded a tape of those early Burl Ives songs (such as "I Know an Old Lady Who Swallowed a Fly") and sent it to him at Base F in Antarctica. Unfortunately, Barrie was unable to play the tape because the tape's speed did not match his player. So he sent it away, with a visiting American, to be transferred. Across the following decades, it was a bitter memory to my dad that the person who did the transfer sent back a tape full of hiss and never returned the original. In all this time Barrie had never been able to hear his friend Ed sing those early songs. As the birthday approached, I called Ed and asked him to bring along his guitar to the party.

Music is a key part of many occasions and get-togethers. It unites people in a way that nothing else can. A good entertainer can focus a roomful of people and direct the ebb and flow of their feelings as they go on a journey into the imagination. It's an amazing thing. No other profession has that sort of uplifting and unifying power. And when Ed got out his guitar, he didn't just sing the songs that Barrie had waited sixty years to hear. His unrehearsed presentation was a captivating mixture of concert and comedy—a nostalgic look back at my father's young life by someone who had known him longer than anyone else. My dad was extremely touched. Perhaps most especially at the moments when Ed and I played together.

But as much as anything, I was struck by Ed's sense of timing for his performance. If he'd started sooner, it would not have been appropriate. Earlier in the party people wanted to talk, get reacquainted, eat and drink. There were gifts to open and a cake to cut. But at some point you could sense a lull. That was the moment when something needed to happen or people would start to leave. That was when I heard Ed say to me, "Shall I take the guitar out now?" I smiled at his entertainer's sense of timing and said, "Yes, now would be perfect."

Walter Kaye, the long-deceased proprietor of our village shop, used to say, "You can only sell something that people want to buy." So true—but as well as having the right product, it pays to put thought and care into the timing of exactly when it is presented.

GETTING "ON" PART I: ACCESSING THE MAGIC

Where we look at the phenomenon of performance energy.

SINCE IT CANNOT be measured, no one can prove it exists. But anyone who has experienced *performance energy* knows it to be as real as the warmth of the sun, a tender kiss or a slap in the face. In my four years of physics study, I developed a specialized understanding of what energy is. In short, energy is everything. It exists as potential energy (such as a ball atop a mountain) or as kinetic energy (a ball rolling downhill). Sound waves, light waves and surf waves are some means by which energy travels. Energy is measurable, and its amount and movement can be described by mathematics. It's a real thing.

So when I got into acting and music, it frustrated me no end that my new acquaintances would discuss energy without any clue what they were saying. It so bugged me to hear these artsy-fartsy types blather on about "energy" when what they were talking about was some metaphysical invention that had no basis in reality. But it's funny how, if you spend enough time with someone's opposing view, you eventually come around to their way of thinking. So over time I changed. But is "energy" even the right word for it? If science can't even detect performance energy, then what business do we have giving it such a name?

I actually think that "energy" is a tremendously good word for what a great performance has. Often we hear of performers being *electric, on fire, shining like a beacon, in the flow, sparking, a smouldering presence, having the power to hold an audience* or simply just being *intense, hot* or *on.*

"That comedian/singer/ukulele player was really *on* tonight," you might say while exiting a show, and everyone would get your meaning. We don't need a smartphone app to tell us when a performance is *on* or *off;* we instinctively just know.

For performers, the state of being *on* is highly desired. If we can get ourselves into the magical realm of *on,* we can do no wrong. Being *on* is like a grand opening of the consciousness where all our practice and rehearsal bypasses our fearful self-critical brain and becomes a servant in a glorious palace of gold, making our performance mightier than we had ever dreamed possible as we find ourselves uplifted, flowing and communicating as one with the audience in a most intimate and connected way. It's nice when it happens. I'm just saying.

It is possible to develop ways of accessing our performance energy, but all the energy in the world won't endow you with skills you never had. So the first part is to know your stuff and get good at what you do. Have confidence in your material and your ability to reproduce that material in a consistent way. Once you're at that point, you're ready to perform with energy.

I read Howard Kaylan's book *Shell Shocked: My Life with The Turtles, Flo and Eddie, and Frank Zappa, Etc…* (by the way, for ukulele content, the book mentions two players, Ian Whitcomb and Tiny Tim). I learned that as well as being the tremendous vocalists on their songs, including "Happy Together" and "Elenore," Howard Kaylan and his musical partner, Mark Volman, provided backing vocals on countless hits by T Rex, Alice Cooper, the Ramones and many others. One time they were recording the vocals for a song called "Hungry Heart" by Bruce Springsteen. Singing in the studio with "The Boss" were Howard, Mark and Steve Van Zandt of the E Street Band.

But there was a problem: when they listened back, someone was singing flat. They returned to the studio floor to try again, but the problem persisted. Howard and Mark were worried. They were being paid big bucks to give "The Boss" world-class backing vocals, and each prayed it wasn't him who was letting Bruce down. Producer Jon Landau called from the control room, "Um, Bruce, you wanna come in here for a second?"

It turned out that Bruce Springsteen was the one singing flat. To rectify the problem, Jon Landau had a surprising idea that shows his instinctive feel for how energy works. He told Bruce to strap on his guitar. The vocals were tried again and everyone was pitch-perfect. You have to realize that Bruce did not *play* the guitar, but his feeling of being "The Boss" returned once he had that axe hanging from his shoulder. This is not an unusual phenomenon. Many musicians find their greatest work happens live, and reproducing it in a studio, without the focus that an audience brings, is next to impossible.

There's something about performing for people that can sharpen us, feed us and give wings to our talents. But we cannot presume it to happen. We also need to create that energy from within and, next, I talk about how to do that.

GETTING "ON" PART 2: ENERGIZING YOUR GIG

Where we look at ways to energize our performances, since audiences can't be relied upon to lift us up and pull us along.

I AM ALWAYS IMPRESSED by actors who can seemingly call up any emotion they care to. I once saw the curtain open on a play to show a man in the middle of a blistering yelling match with his (offstage) partner. The scene certainly grabbed my attention, and I can only imagine what the actor must have gone through to prepare himself to be in such a state. It's an extreme example of the kind of thing that all performers need to be able to do. Here are some ways to access your energy.

- ***Prepare for what you're about to do.*** Mentally transform yourself into the onstage you. Find out what helps you to rise to the occasion. Most performers find a quiet sense of inner focus before releasing their energy. This may be done by sitting in a quiet room, going for a walk or finding our inner quiet amidst a crowd. The very act of dressing can be a mental preparation that forces us to slow down and focus.
- ***Be the boss.*** You need to be in charge of the room. Some people do this more readily than others, but I am living proof that the ability can be developed even by someone who is relatively shy. The boss is confident in his abilities while being aware of his limitations. The boss is free to try out ideas and isn't afraid to make mistakes. The boss is well prepared but knows that if mistakes are made, they also have skills to turn the situation around. The boss is adept at making others feel at ease. Whatever the boss says or does is right. That is real freedom.

Attaining such a level of "bossness" is a long-term process of personal confidence building. Experience is important. What works for you in one venue may be ineffective somewhere else. There's a resilience that comes from the repeated practice of putting yourself out there and shaping your environment.

- ***Channel someone great.*** In my first book, *The Ukulele Entertainer,* I talked about "channelling" other performers. If you see yourself as an unworthy nobody that no one in their right mind would want to watch, try being someone else instead. Most great performers have constructed onstage personalities that are larger and less complicated than their real selves. Play around with this idea at home. Think of someone well known whom you admire, and act out how they would do your show.

  By introducing and singing your songs as someone else, you give yourself the feeling of being a *somebody* who is *larger than life.* Notice what differences there are between this borrowed persona and the way you normally perform. Do you like the new you? You can choose to keep some aspects and drop others as you move towards creating your onstage self.
- ***Avoid stimulants.*** "Dutch courage" (alcohol) may reduce nervousness, but it also affects the ability to think. It's not a clever trade-off, especially if you have lyrics, chords and other stage work to remember. Similarly, other drugs that performers use to help them perform better in one area usually negatively affect some other area. So I don't recommend them. Not even caffeine. I know of bands whose members drink wine and coffee to get a pre-stage buzz, but I find adrenalin is quite enough to get the job done, thank you. Performers who jumpstart themselves with lots of caffeine tend to come across as slightly insane rather than filled with energy.

  It's no fun to be high and onstage when paranoia or some other fear kicks in. I once heard Carlos Santana in a radio interview talk about playing his song "Soul Sacrifice" at Woodstock. Most of us hear that piece and think what great musicianship it is, but Santana hears it as very raw. He and most, or all, of the band were high on mescaline. So did he enjoy performing at Woodstock? No, he did not. His abiding memory is terror. As he played he was praying to God to get him through the experience, promising never to perform like this again. I don't judge those who use chemical stimulants to perform. And sometimes the trade-off in a given situation may be worth it. But long-term use tends to be problematic.

- ***Focus your energy.*** Imagine a hose shooting a powerful jet of water in a single direction. Now imagine that same hose dropped to the floor and spraying water around in every direction. Obviously the first scenario is the one that delivers real power. Holding your energy in stillness will often keep the attention of your audience better than twitching, pacing, jerking and generally throwing yourself around. The sense of possibility, the feeling of *anything could happen* is often more effective than physical activity. This was brought home to me once watching a barbershop quartet singing contest. The judges gave more presentation points to a quartet of heavy-set men who barely moved than to four supple and skinny guys with clever and well-rehearsed movements. It was a valuable demonstration of "Less is more." Whether you choose to move around or not, do it with focus and attention. Make your energy one-directional and aim its full force at the audience.
- ***Ignore the ego.*** If in the middle of a song you hear your inner voice saying, "I am really nailing this one. There's going to be a standing ovation for sure," don't be surprised if the song ends to a less than lukewarm smattering of applause. Conversely, you might feel awkward and unsure of what you're doing, only to later discover that the audience found the performance extremely moving. That great actor's actor Laurence Olivier once sat in his dressing room after receiving overwhelming adulation from what had been an incredible performance. Another actor asked what he'd done to elicit such a moving response. Olivier responded with bewildered grief, "I don't know." Sometimes all we can do is develop our art and present it the best way we can. What the audience feels, if anything at all, is entirely out of our hands.
- ***Take a chance.*** I've often observed that the first performance of a song can be the best ever (see page 79). Doing material you're not entirely

comfortable with seems to generate sparks that oft-repeated material doesn't. Perhaps something in our focus or body language gives the sense of walking a tightrope that the audience picks up on. So be brave: don't be afraid to try something new.

- ***Perform as if everyone is having a fantastic time—and they will!*** I perform outdoor street shows at the Granville Island Public Market, where off-season crowds can be hard to come by. At such times you may occasionally see me performing to empty benches on the periphery of the market square. As people bustle by and glance my way I wonder if they think, *Who is that loser of a musician without an audience?* I deal with this by making jokes, bantering with passers-by and introducing my songs as if the benches were groaning under the weight of happy onlookers. I truly believe that doing so makes me appear cheerful and interesting and not nearly as deranged as you might suppose. Very soon, like the grit at the centre of a pearl, people begin to stop and form the nucleus of a gathering audience.

Performers deliver escape and fantasy, so be free to create an imaginary world and make it real for you. When you do this successfully, the audience will gladly buy into and share your reality. And remember: As performers we have immense energy. That's why we're called stars.

FAILING (TO SUCCEED!!)

Where I suggest that there are important lessons to be learned from performance bloopers we'd rather forget.

WE ALL TRY to succeed. And when it comes to performing, we aim for success all the time. Failure is so hard to take. I've known people who vowed never to perform again after suffering humiliation through misspoken words, forgotten music or some other embarrassment. Why do we persist in an art form where errors are made in public and catcalls are as likely as curtain calls? Myself, I've bounced back from more humiliating failures than I care to recall—some so traumatic their memory still dredges a groan from my solar plexus region. Here's a reluctantly offered example, and excuse me if I shudder.

My career as a solo entertainer began early in 1991 as Ralph the Clown. Wishing to be "different," I avoided the traditional red nose. Instead my makeup was a light flesh base with red lips and red around my eyes, surrounded by large white circles edged in black. I thought it was pretty innovative. In a guitar case I carried all my props, which included magic tricks, juggling balls, a Suzuki ukulele, face paint, balloons and Yorick (a rubber skull with moveable jaw). It was my second gig and I was the roving entertainer at a large indoor mall. I was entertaining three young children when a hysterical woman shot towards me. I can't remember her exact words, but they went something like "Who are you? What are you doing with these children only yards from the exit doors? Where are their parents?"

Explaining that I was a clown hired by the mall only made things worse. Staring aghast at my face she said, "You're not a clown, you don't look like a clown, and"—pointing to Yorick—"what's *that?*" With his bouncing rubber jaw, Yorick had been amusing the kids with his take on life as a disembodied skull. But I was too crushed to explain further. She told me to get away from the children before heading off to report me to the mall authorities.

Wandering disconsolately back through the mall, I looked up and recoiled in further shock as I saw a frightening figure coming towards me. It took a moment before I realized it was my own reflection. My makeup, although fine in the bathroom mirror, was morbidly ghoulish at a distance. I recognized how my appearance, my proximity to exit doors, three parentless children and a talking skull presented a startling constellation of worrying signals. I imagined a newspaper headline: Little Mall of Horrors—Woman Warns Parents Beware of Skull Clown. I felt ready to quit. Once home, I told this to my agent, who was unperturbed. "Don't worry, Ralph, have a beer. Relax, it'll be fine." And it was—except for a shudder that comes over me every time I recall that day.

The experience taught me several vital and, in retrospect, fairly obvious dos and don'ts for entertaining. The next day I created a new look. It included a humble red nose, and I'd never again be mistaken for anything but a clown.

I see the creation of a performer as being somewhat like sculpting. When the young Michelangelo started carving the already blocked-out statue of David, he must have sensed the perfection that lay within the marble. But only by chipping away at the excess could he reveal the beauty within. The discarding of unwanted material is akin to the choices made after our performance screw-ups. The removal of that which does not serve us guides us towards greater perfection.

We think of performance success as being perfectly played songs followed by loud audience approval. And that is a wonderful thing. But it doesn't teach us much. Far richer is the cataclysmic failure, its stark lesson shining bright light on the parts we need to improve, guiding us through the dark to more glorious horizons than our imaginations ever conceived.

In reality most of our shows lie somewhere between all-out success and irrevocable mishap. It's up to us to enjoy the highlights while transforming disaster into future applause. In other words, success is no more than success, but failure is a means to greater glory. In Yorkshire, where I'm from, there's a saying: "Where there's muck there's brass." Which means: Glittering treasure can be found in that which appears worthless.

MANAGING YOUR PRE-SHOW TERROR

Your small show went well. But now you've been called to perform at a more extravagant event than you've ever played before, and the idea of this is terrifying.

THE PHONE CALL goes something like this. "I was in the audience at the Sheep Shearers Social above the Little Taj Restaurant last week, and I just thought you were fantastic. We'd love to have you come and entertain at our annual Gala of Glitter and Stars Extravaganza in the Sinatra Show Lounge next Valentine's Day. I've told the other board members how wonderful you are and we sure hope you can make it, because I think our audience would get a real kick out of you."

It's a call that can strike terror into the heart of a performer who is on their way up. On one hand, it's the sort of opportunity you've been waiting for for years. On the other hand, you are well aware of your own inconsistency. Your heart knows that while some of your shows go really well, some still flop, and you haven't acquired enough experience to deal with the many unexpected situations that can break your stride and mess up your show. But you say yes to the gig. And that's when pre-show adrenalin starts to become a part of your life.

Non-performers think that stage fright is something that only happens in the minutes before going onstage. But more experienced performers know that show anxiety, even panic, can begin long before that—sometimes months before the show in question.

Can we use pre-show adrenalin to our advantage, and what do we do when it gets to be too much? Here are some strategies from someone who's been there.

USING FEAR TO YOUR ADVANTAGE

Once, at a performance class I was teaching, a woman told me her story from college days of how she had been virtually traumatized by a stage appearance. Thinking she'd signed up for a minor-league talent show, she arrived with a guitar and a half-learned song to discover the performance was in front of hundreds of people. It's the stuff that nightmares are made of. She was mortified with tension—which the audience picked up on and reflected back to her in their postures. She said the audience looked as tense and anxious as she felt. In the middle of the song, however, she messed up a difficult chord and loudly muttered, "Shit!" At which point the audience spontaneously laughed with combined relief.

Although she survived the experience, she was left with a long-term fear of the stage. In the class we discussed the paradox of how musicians, sensitive to emotions, are often more afflicted by conflict and traumatic situations than the average person, often making it all the harder for them to get onstage.

If you have a performance looming, it's a great idea to anticipate the fear-filled stage situation while at home. Instead of practising your songs on the living-room couch like you usually do, set up a microphone. Imagine being announced and walking onstage. What do you do next? What do you say? Imagine hundreds of eyes on you. Make it so real that you actually get scared and mess up. How do you recover? Do you come up with something spontaneous that helps to cover the mistake and move on with the show? Whatever it is, write it down because you may want to use it later.

Doing your show at home with your eyes closed can be a powerful way to imagine that you are really there. Allow the fear to come and when it does, deal with it. Discover that you have the inner resources to get through situations where your mind wants to shut down. Eventually, when you perform for real, you will still have fear, but that feeling will be accompanied by the knowledge that you've handled this before and can move on successfully.

ELIMINATING UNWANTED FEAR

When the fear gets too much it can lead to sleepless nights, anxiety and panic attacks. My best suggestion to overcome the debilitating effects of mental fear is to move. Get outside into the natural light and fresh air. Running (or brisk walking) is a great way to get your body moving, your feet pounding and your breath deepening. As your body loosens up, your mind works things out, sees things in perspective and comes up with new ideas to help your situation.

I have also found that doing yoga at home, especially with a video, is a good way to get out of your mind and into your body. Kundalini yoga is helpful for this because it uses repeated movements (often quite vigorous), rather than held poses, and is a great distraction for the mind.

If you're in a situation where moving is impossible, then take about ten slow deep breaths. This works wonders for soothing raging emotions, whether they be extreme anger or paralyzing fear.

Eventually, performance fear may disappear completely. But until then study it. Find out what feeds it. What makes fear grow and what causes it to diminish in your mind? Get comfortable with having fear around as if it were a troublesome, but still loved, family member. Discover ways to disarm it and remove its power over you.

BANISH STAGE FRIGHT

Performing in public can trigger our mind-body defence system to react as if it were facing the equivalent of an enemy attack. But there is hope.

By age ten I'd experienced both the agony and the ecstasy of performance. These early experiences taught me that fear can be a powerful, yet ultimately controllable force. My stage career did not begin well. At age eight I was Father Christmas in the school play. Suited in a fragile outfit made from ultra-thin 1970s plastic, I was completely *un*suited to the role. I remember adults imploring me to "Skip happily." But my performance was lacklustre and joyless. Afterwards, although I'd been warned over and over again, "Be careful with the suit," it tore down the middle. My misery complete, I burst into tears. If not for the kindness of Mrs. Eleanor—teaching assistant, piano player, part-time tear-wiper and suit-mender—I might never have walked onstage again.

Two years later I sported a charcoal beard and tricorn hat in the role of Long John Silver. I played the part to the hilt, oohing and aahrring and grimacing lopsidedly. I even had realistic muskets to wave. They'd been hand-carved by my dad and accessorized with bits of old typewriter for a trigger and a hammer. After each show I basked in the approval of friends, parents and teachers. It felt very good.

Such conflicting experiences help to explain the bipolar feelings—abject terror and great joy—that performing has brought me. When the experience is more about terror than joy, it's called stage fright.

The effects of the fight or flight response are similar for everyone. Faced with a threatening situation, our system sends a surge of adrenalin through our body, resulting in increased blood flow to the parts needed for self-defence—the hands, feet and brain. Heart rate quickens and temperature rises, causing sweaty hands and brow. The increased need for oxygen leads to quicker breathing, perhaps hyperventilating. Meanwhile the entire digestive system shuts down, leading to nausea, cramping in the stomach and dry mouth as the salivary glands temporarily stop functioning. Eventually our body decides it would be better off relying on instinct alone for survival and consequently takes the seemingly drastic action of shutting down the thinking process altogether.

How strange that these over-the-top physical consequences occur for something as benign as singing and playing ukulele for people. I mean, shutting down the ability to think? Really! Here are nine suggestions to help eliminate stage fear.

▸ ***Prepare and practise.*** Preparation lifts the mental load from your brain and reduces stress. Anything that can be done ahead of time should be. Decide on your songs, choose your outfit, get your hair done, put gas in the car, allow plenty of time to get to the gig, and have instruments and other essential equipment packed.

This spring I was invited to perform one of my newer and wordier songs at another performer's sold-out show. I thought I knew the song inside out, but ended up forgetting some words in a spot where I'd never messed up before. I have an (unproven) theory that to truly know a song inside out you need to have flunked every line. Make those mistakes in rehearsal or they'll happen onstage. Many new performers attempt to perform songs from memory before they're ready. So keep working on it. Really knowing your stuff helps your confidence more than anything else.

- ***Use visualization.*** Imagining a successful show is something you can do long before show day. Get your mind used to the idea of what is going to happen. That way it won't be such a shock when the real thing happens. As you rehearse, imagine you are performing for a real audience.
- ***Perform every chance you can get.*** Performing is the act of doing a familiar activity in an unusual situation. Playing music alone is very different from doing it for hundreds on a stage through a PA. The only way to make performing into a "normal" occurrence is to get out there and perform every chance you can.
- ***Exercise and spend time in nature.*** Days or weeks before a show, run, cycle or walk in the most natural surroundings you can find. The natural world is a soothing balm for the mind and provides a relaxing place to mentally go over any issues that trouble you. It's also a great idea to memorize lyrics while moving.
- ***Let a little fear be your friend.*** Know that fear can work to your advantage. Whereas overwhelming dread causes blanking, a smaller amount of adrenalin sharpens the mind and hones the instincts, perhaps creating your best possible performance.
- ***Use reversal theory.*** According to reversal theory, it's possible to use your body to change your mindset. In other words, if you behave confidently, your mind responds by thinking confidently. This works. Find it within yourself to stand tall. Relax your shoulders. Look people in the eye and give a firm handshake. Be powerful. When you come from a place of strength, others will respond to you in kind. This is part of your preparation as you make your way to the performance space. Work towards being confident, in control, and eager to get out there and get on with it.
- ***Alleviate the physical issues.*** Breathe! When you are fearful, take a dozen deep slow breaths. Your brain and body need oxygen to deal with the

situation, so supply it. For your dry mouth, take sips of water and massage around and under the jaw to stimulate saliva flow. Use lip balm so your lips don't feel dry and uncomfortable.

- ***Occupy your right brain.*** In the middle of a song when your brain starts telling you you're about to forget the lyrics, find something to focus on. Study the chandelier or count the pictures on the wall. This keeps the right brain busy so the left brain can continue with its job of delivering the words.
- ***Know the venue and prepare up to the last minute.*** Every gig has unknown quantities. So make a pre-show visit to the space. Stand on the stage and imagine the audience. Once at the show, observe the crowd. Get a feel for the people; gauge their mood and notice what they respond to. Make last-minute refinements to what you will say and do.

It's great when everything goes well. But it doesn't always. With so many variables, it's impossible to prepare for everything. That's why experienced professional performers have *riders*. Riders are add-ons to their contract that specify everything from the food and drink in the dressing room to the layout of audience seating. It's all done to eliminate unwelcome surprises. Here are two examples:

RIDER FOR FATHER CHRISTMAS

- Milk and cookies in dressing room
- Pad of paper and pen for making lists
- Mini snacks and small furniture for elf assistant
- Security staff must ensure the audience consists of only good boys and girls
- Separate designated washrooms for reindeer

RIDER FOR LONG JOHN SILVER

- Two bottles of grog in dressing room
- Large bowl of treasure with pieces of eight removed

- Parrot food (good quality, i.e., not sweepings from the pet shop floor)
- Complimentary sachets of anti-slip powder for peg leg

YOUR FIRST PA

Buying and using your own public address system, or PA, can be a daunting prospect. Here's some help from one non-techie (me) to another (that would be you).

BEING AT THE mercy of other people's bad sound systems can be funny but is rarely fun. A friend of mine, Paul Latta, runs a Las Vegas–style Polynesian dance company. His tales of bad PAs that his clients have supplied (usually to avoid paying to rent professional sound gear) are quite hilarious. My favourite is the time he arrived at a gig and the client handed him a child's My First Sony CD player. To avoid such situations, it can be beneficial to get your own gear. Herewith some guidance:

WHAT IS A PA EXACTLY?

PA, sound system and amp are fairly interchangeable terms meaning *equipment that makes you louder.*

PAs or sound systems can have multiple components, including microphones, a mixer, an amplifier, monitor speakers and main speakers, which all connect by cables. You don't really need all that stuff. An amp (this is general shorthand for an amplifier that includes a speaker plus inputs for a couple of microphones) is a single device that usually does the job.

WHAT DO I NEED?

Think about your requirements. The average ukulele entertainer needs a PA that is:

- ***Loud enough*** to be heard at most of the gigs you expect to be doing.
- ***As natural sounding as possible.*** What comes out of the speaker should be like your acoustic sound only louder.

- ***Reasonably portable.*** Think about how you travel to gigs. Will the PA fit in your vehicle? Can it be carried by bike, bus or on the plane?
- ***Reasonably priced.*** Generally, the more you pay, the better you sound.
- ***Simple to use.*** Forget any piece of equipment that is so complex you feel you need a master's degree in acoustic arts to work it.

WHAT IS AVAILABLE?

The good news is that many PA companies now sell portable amps tailor-made for independent small-scale performers. Just plug in your microphones, adjust the sound controls and sing. These amps require little expertise, are reasonably priced and sometimes have a built-in battery for outdoor gigs where no electricity is available.

HOW MUCH SHOULD I SPEND?

An "okay" sounding amp can cost two or three hundred dollars. That was my budget twelve years ago when I went shopping for an amp at my local music shop. Rob, the owner, insisted on showing me an amp made by the German company AER (Audio Electric Research) that had just come in. The sound was clean and powerful and without distortion at loud volume, and the amp could be lifted with one hand. It was also five times over my budget, but I knew right away I had to get it. To pay for it, I sold all my multi-component gear. It was a purchase I never regretted. The new amp was an improvement over the old PA in every way. I'm not necessarily saying that AER is what you should get. Look around: these days there are more choices and prices have come down. Try out a few and see what works for you.

WHAT DO ALL THOSE KNOBS AND BUTTONS DO?

To illustrate this, here is a drawing of the control panel of a typical guitar amp (cross out the word *guitar* and write in *ukulele* if it makes you feel better). The amp has two main sections, called Channel 1 and Channel 2:

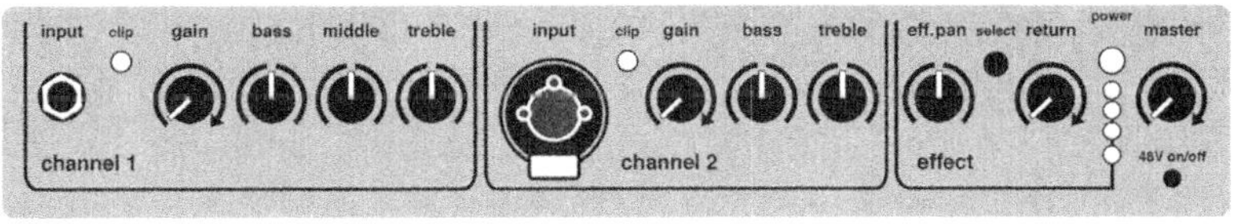

- ***Channel 1.*** If your instrument has a built-in electric pickup, plug the ¼-inch cord from your instrument into the Channel 1 Input. If your uke doesn't have a pickup, you'll need to play the uke into a microphone. But there's a small problem there, because most microphone cables have an XLR connector (a chunky connector with three pins), and your instrument input is for a ¼-inch cable. So you may need to get an XLR to ¼-inch adapter to plug your instrument microphone into the ¼-inch socket.
- ***Channel 2.*** This is for your vocal microphone. You can see that this input takes the XLR three-pin connector from a standard microphone cable.
- ***Gain.*** Each channel has a Gain control, meaning that your instrument and voice each have their own volume knobs. When turning on the amp, always start with each Gain and the Master volume set at zero. Increase the levels slowly so you don't blow your speaker. Turn up the Master a little and then adjust each Gain so voice and ukulele are in good balance. Then turn up the total volume to the required level using the Master.
- ***Clip.*** If a Clip light is coming on, then your Gain is set too high. So turn down the Gain and increase the Master volume. If it happens that your Master is turned up full, your Clip light is on and you're still not loud enough—it's time for a bigger amp.
- ***EQ Controls (Equalization).*** Bass, middle and treble are used to adjust the frequencies of your sound. Set them to the centre position. Listen to your sound. Is it too tinny? Then turn down the treble a little (or turn up the middle). Too boomy, then turn down the bass. Different rooms and different crowds require different EQ settings. If possible, get someone with experience to stand in the audience and inform you what adjustments should be made. If you're not sure, keep them centred.

- ***Effects.*** Some amps have effects built into them. The most common two are reverb and echo. I rarely use echo myself, but reverb is good to have since it fills out your sound (like singing in the shower) and that's good—up to a point. The Return knob changes the amount of the effect. But keep it subtle: if it's turned up to where people *notice* you've added reverb, then it's too high.

  The eff. (effects) pan allows you to put more effect onto either your voice or your instrument. Having the knob in the centre puts an equal amount of effect on each channel.
- ***Phantom Power.*** The 48v on/off button is also known as phantom power. Some (but not all) condenser microphones need an external electric power source to make them work, and this is the button you press if you need that.

Not all amps are exactly as described here. You'll find every PA has its own idiosyncrasies to figure out, so don't be afraid to learn on the job.

Having your own gear will add to your performing confidence. Many facilities, such as restaurants, community centres and retirement homes, for example, may boast that they have a PA for you to use. But be wary and ask questions—it may be a My First Sony!

MAKE BETTER ONLINE VIDEOS—PLEASE

Here are some basic ideas to make your online music videos more watchable.

In the run-up to a local festival, I helped judge two dozen entries in the categories of Best Original Song, Best Cover Song and Best Ensemble Song. It was my first time judging such a competition, and separating the qualities of songwriting, singing ability, performance and videography to come up with a grade that fairly represented the videos was a challenge.

There were many talented performances, but the truth is that nearly every video contained flaws that could so easily have been avoided. So I've come up with a list of things you can do to make your videos, if not great, then at least more watchable.

- ***Beware of hats.*** When Britain's Prince William came to Canada, he was presented with a handsome white cowboy hat. Did he put it on his head right away and grin for the cameras? No, he did not. And there's a good reason for that. Hats can give you character and presence, but they can also make a person appear foolish, creepy or just plain crazy. This is especially true in low-quality videos shot with bad lighting, because hats cast shadows that hide your eyes. Hats can work, but make sure your chosen cranial covering supports your performance rather than serves as a distraction. Later on in their Canada tour, William, Kate and the coach driver wore cowboy hats for a carefully planned photo opportunity and they looked great.
- ***Find good sound balance.*** In many of the contest videos, the ukulele was so loud it overpowered the vocal. Since many singers aren't enunciating too well to begin with, this makes it very hard to hear lyrics. Think of the ukulele as your backing instrument. Got an electric uke? Avoid using it. The sound of cheap pickups coming through computer speakers is often poor, tinny and way too loud. Position the recorder so your voice is the primary feature, and use the natural acoustic sound of your instrument.
- ***Sing clearly and well.*** You may think it adds character to mush up the words, but I for one have little tolerance for a song whose lyrics can't be made out. Also work in vocal techniques such as dynamics, vibrato (see page 48) and phrasing to make the song more interesting to listeners.
- ***Think about your location, wardrobe and camera angles.*** There are many ways to look weird and eccentric, and you probably want to avoid most of them. Imagine how your video will look to others, and ask yourself, "Is this how I want the rest of the world to see me long into the future?"

- ***Make eye contact. Communicate.*** Looking away to one side, up in the air or down at your feet sends a mixed message. It's as if you're saying, "I have something important to tell you, so excuse me while I focus my attention somewhere else entirely." Relate to the camera as you would to a person.
- ***Create emotion and playfulness.*** This is what makes your video worth watching. As viewers we're not expecting a flawless performance. But as we view your work we do yearn for a glimpse, however brief, of your humanity. So show us who you are. Entertain us. Make us laugh, cry or wonder. Exactly how you achieve this is your call, but work on it *before* you power up the camera. Don't believe for a moment that the camera will create the magic for you. Take a risk and do something a little outside your comfort zone (but keep your clothes on. Sheesh).
- ***Do many takes.*** Be honest with yourself. Notice any problems your video has. Solve the issues and try again.
- ***And... smile!!*** Remember, you're making a music video, not defusing a bomb.

REGARDING HATS

What? You don't agree that "hats can make a person appear foolish, creepy or just plain crazy"? Please allow me to clarify my position.

MY COMMENTS ABOUT wearing hats in online videos bothered some people. In fact, because of me, some readers no longer perform in a hat. "Because I know you don't like hats, Ralph," they say in an accusing tone, as if I'm responsible for spoiling their fun. Others tell me that despite my anti-hat stance, they continue to sing in a hat.

I feel slightly guilty for having burst a few blissful bubbles of heady ignorance. But the reactions are understandable.

Hats are personal. In 1981 a group of high-spirited youths entered a Yorkshire pub wherein an old fellow in a flat cap sat at the bar contemplating his glass of stout. One of the youths (not me), in a moment of abandon, grabbed the cap off the old man's head, put it on his own head and beamed round at his mates with amusement. What he didn't see was the old man slowly winding up for a massive punch. Since everybody but the offending youth could see what was about to happen, he was the only surprised party when the octogenarian's fist connected with the side of his head. And what was the unspoken consensus of the witnesses in the pub? The kid had it coming. Violence is out of line for most types of insult, but you just don't mess with other people's hats.

Nevertheless, while I stand by my views on the risks of wearing hats while performing, I feel I should qualify my position.

If you're a performer, you want people to remember you. Therefore you need to display an appealing and consistent product. We are our own billboards. Each of us is a pitch-person for our own talent as we hawk and hustle to get others to buy into what we have to offer. Your performance garb should align with both your stage personality and your music. If you sing rockabilly songs dressed in a nun's habit, people will demand clarification. Great entertainers go to great lengths to look the part. Even those appearing not to care about how they look still make a clear statement (for example late-'80s grunge musicians wore grungy clothes not because they didn't care, but because that was their chosen look).

As salespeople of ourselves, our heads are our trademark. The area on and around our faces is the most watched part of us. So whether you go for long, spiky or afro, in the case of hair, or choose a topper, trilby or toque as a hat, I suggest you think carefully about what you wish to portray. Elvis Presley knew this. Ever see him with mussed up hair? No. That's because his hair was his hat. His dyed black, slicked back hairdo was the most consistent item worn throughout his career.

You may have to experiment or you won't know what bandana, beret or beehive will work for you. But my suggestion is to think about it awhile before deciding it's a grand idea to go onstage wearing your Fred's Fast Trucking baseball cap, or some distended lump of felt resembling an unidentifiable fungus.

When I first began performing, I adopted the bowler hat (that's a *derby* to Americans). I wore one at every show for about fifteen years. It broadcast my Britishness before speaking and gave the audience an immediate sense of connection with what I offered. I eventually stopped wearing the bowler for practical reasons: (1) it gets hot in warm weather; and (2) it's a difficult item to travel with. Protecting a good hat takes special care. And the limitations airlines place on bags made my bowler an unfeasible, and unfoldable, accessory.

I'm not the type to wear an eye-catching hat everywhere I go. But doing so can offer advantages. Grammy-winning musician and farmer Keoki Kahumoku on the Big Island of Hawaii has a hat that he wears both onstage and off. It appears to be a reworked felt cowboy hat with the hatband removed. It's a slightly unusual look and at the same time quite brilliant, for it, along with his beard, makes him immediately recognizable. I visited Keoki and he took me to see an experimental aquaculture farm that works to obtain high produce yields using the water from tanks of live fish as fertilizer. A talk was in progress and even though we were still some distance away, the person giving the talk suddenly stopped her presentation on noticing Keoki's unmistakable outline.

"Hi Keoki! Ladies and gentlemen, allow me to introduce you to Keoki Kahumoku," she shouted while waving enthusiastically in our direction. I suddenly realized my friend was a celebrity. Keoki was brought to the front, where he gave an impromptu and extremely interesting speech about the importance of sustainable agriculture. Keoki is neither the first nor the last to understand the importance of headwear as a recognition tool.

Unlike with Keoki, the theatre performer's stage personality is usually completely separate from their civilian appearance. And there are others, like myself, who comfortably live in both worlds. In my case I rarely perform or teach without a bowtie, although it's a look you probably wouldn't see me sporting while walking around my neighbourhood. Thinking about it, the bowtie, being close to my face, functions as a sort of reverse hat. Characteristic facial hair (think ZZ Top, Frank Zappa and Colonel Sanders) also does this, as does an unusual pair of spectacles. (Buddy Holly's optician solved Buddy's problem of not being able to see onstage by suggesting he try some distinctively eye-catching frames—and it's easy to see what that did for his career.)

So forgive me if my comment caused you to part from your precious hat. I was only trying to be helpful. It's all about finding something that suits you and improves—rather than detracts from—your stage performance. In the end my hat truly goes off to *anyone* with the courage to perform in public.

THE BOWTIE MANIFESTO

A performer must dress well, and few items of clothing make a bigger statement than the little bowtie.

TROY IS A lawyer. A lawyer is a type of entertainer whose job it is to perform without the aid of a ukulele. This is why they're paid so much. I last saw Troy about ten years ago over drinks in a hotel lounge. I was wearing my performing get-up, which has always included a bowtie.

I never forgot our conversation that day, as Troy lamented how he didn't have the personality to wear a bowtie. He knew an older and respected lawyer who always wore a bowtie, but Troy knew that he himself had neither the confidence nor gravitas to pull it off. His sentiment stayed with me. I wondered, "How does an item of clothing as innocuous as a bowtie hold so much power that someone would be afraid to wear it?"

Whenever I meet a fellow bowtie wearer I always say "Hello" and find out about their attraction to this unusual item of neckwear. Everyone has a story. An antiques shop owner in Australia told me he's worn one daily since the age of seven. His sister was visiting one time and as he came downstairs without his bowtie on, his sister took one look and burst into tears. She couldn't remember ever seeing him without a bowtie.

David Hilton in Eugene, Oregon, has always attended my shows in a bowtie. We've spent hours talking about the effect bowties have on people. We love the fact that when you wear a bowtie, it makes people smile. Although not everyone feels that way. I once wore one for my dad's birthday party and he frowned when he saw me, saying I looked like a salesman—which I suppose is what all entertainers are, in a sense—but the idea that a bowtie can make one appear both charming *and* an untrustworthy purveyor of snake oil surprised me. It's a complex and mysterious clothing accessory. I don't wear one every day, but I consider it an indispensable part of my performance attire that many people have come to associate with me as part of my *look*.

Professional musicians need merchandise to sell at performances. Often the pay we get for gigs barely covers the cost of touring, and the sale of T-shirts, CDs and other paraphernalia keeps us in business. So David and I decided it was high time that a "Ralph Shaw Bowtie" became available to my masses of fans. I considered this idea for a year without finding a way to make such an item affordable. "Who would buy a $40 bowtie at a concert?" I thought.

It was Victoria Vox who gave me the answer. Victoria has pulled off a succession of quirky promotional ideas (her most memorable being the screen-printed underwear she sells at her concerts). I told her about my unworkable bowtie idea and she had an immediate solution for me. "Make it out of paper," she said.

And that's what I've done (it's thin card, actually). My graphic designing, uke-playing friend Jen Chang and I came up with a foldable make-your-own bowtie kit using artwork from another uke player, Roan Shankaruk.

My bowtie was proudly unveiled at the first Canada Ukes Ukulele Festival (a.k.a. Weekend at Ralph's). It was an utter delight to see so many people buying, making and wearing my newest and most unusual item of *Merch*. Interestingly, it seemed to be an even bigger hit with the ladies than with the men, and one little sweetie (Macy) who had never seen a bowtie naturally assumed it was to be worn in the hair—this works too!

As for Troy the lawyer, I happened to bump into him recently in the very same hotel lounge and he was wearing a bowtie. He'd just won an important case that day and was having a beverage to celebrate. I reminded him about our bowtie conversation from a decade before. Funny thing, he had no memory of that day but he told me he *always* wears a bowtie to work now. It was a big moment for me to hear him say that. Troy the lawyer has come into his own. His confidence has grown and his gravitas is big enough to sport a bowtie. Amazing.

MY BOWTIE MANIFESTO

START ATTRACTING SMILES

There are many reasons to wear a bowtie. It completes an outfit and makes it sing. To dress well is to own your self-respect, and this in turn brings respect from others. People are more likely to remember you. Heads turn and strangers smile at you. A bowtie says you are a fun person who has many ways to charm.

WHO CAN WEAR A BOWTIE?

Now, I'm not saying a bowtie will make you into a somebody, but I do say you have to be a somebody to wear a bowtie. Think of it like a monarch's crown or Batman's cape: not everyone can wear one with ease. You need to have a certain amount of gravitas and self-confidence or you could end up feeling like a dork. At the very least you should be comfortable in your own skin.

SHOULD A WOMAN WEAR A BOWTIE?

But of course! A funky outfit that includes a bowtie will enhance a woman's inherent femininity in a cool and offbeat way that will delight others. So, whoever you are, express yourself in whatever way you feel.

BE A BOWTIE WEARING BABE/BOY MAGNET

A bowtie sets you apart and makes you special. People who might otherwise ignore you may start calling you "Sir" or "Madam." A bowtie can be a powerful babe or boy magnet. Who wouldn't want to spend time with someone whose bowtie demonstrates that they are a joyful, well-dressed, clean and fun-loving individual with a zest for living?

WITH A GREAT BOWTIE COMES GREAT RESPONSIBILITY

When wearing your bowtie out in public, remember to hold your head high, enjoy those around you and above all, smile! Few sights are more depressing than a sad bowtie wearer.

CHOOSE YOUR BOWTIE CAREFULLY

Some bowties are subtle. Others are large and colourful, as if they're screaming HEY, LOOK AT ME!!! So choose carefully. Before you leave the house, pick a bowtie that matches how you wish to transform your world. For transform it you will. People snap out of their humdrum little lives. They forget their problems and want to know more about you. It's a wonderful life, and a bowtie will help you get more out of it with minimal effort.

SO WEAR A BOWTIE AND LIVE NOW!

P.S. And, in case you're wondering: *bow tie*, *bowtie* and *bow-tie* are all correct spellings.

THE ECONOMICS OF ENTERTAINMENT

Where we look at the realities of making a living as a ukulele entertainer.

ARE YOU CURIOUS about making a living as a musical performer? It's a subject that those of us doing it don't discuss too much, since the reality is often at odds with what we want people to see. So I'll just yank back the curtain here—*swish*—and let the enlightenment begin.

Why do we do it? The work of an entertainer is too unpredictable to be a job, too ungrounded to be a career and too financially insecure to be a business. It's a calling. You have to *want* to do it. Sometimes I conjure up more financially stable and less mentally stressful ways of earning a living, but in the end I can't imagine doing anything else.

I know there are many professions far more arduous than mine, but can there be a more misunderstood way of life than that of a performer? People see me smiling and well-dressed and tell me I'm so lucky to do what I love. And they're right—I do love my work—but here's why I don't recommend life as an entertainer to anyone.

▸ ***The pay is less than you think and the work is harder than it looks.*** Countless unpaid and unseen hours go into the preparation of each show. So it's ironic when, after a successful performance, there's a certain look I get from a client as they hand over the cheque. Slightly resentful, the look says, "You were laughing, playing the ukulele and having such a good time. Heck, we even fed you. Now on top of all that I have to pay you?!" The client doesn't realize how hard it is for a performer to get up in front of an unknown group of strangers and befriend them. Most occupations outside of the service industry don't depend on cheerfulness, but we do expect our servers to smile, and if an entertainer isn't having a good time, then how can the audience be expected to? I confess I have evenings when staying home would be preferable to cranking up my energy and adrenalin levels. But, as they say, the show must go on.

- ***It costs money to make money.*** One evening at Napa's Wine Country 'Ukulele Festival, I commented to a local person how lavish the winery was where I'd just played. She responded, "You can make a small fortune in the wine business—so long as you start with a large one." That can also be said of the music business. I didn't start with a large or a small fortune. But I did have ample reserves of naiveté, blind faith and ignorance—plus the energy and willingness to learn on the job.

  Here's the thing: when you become an entertainer, you need to figure out what sort of performer you're going to be. Then you create marketing materials—websites, printed matter, videos, song clips, even a newsletter—in order to reach the people who pay you. It's as if you had to apply for your job *every day that you go to work.*

  Being a performer is expensive and all kinds of things can mess up your plans. For example, years ago I decided to become a guest entertainer on cruise ships. Getting this job required a promo video of my show being performed with a ten-piece orchestra. To this end I paid thousands to a band arranger, who wrote musical scores that I could hand to any cruise ship orchestra. Suddenly, with the 2008 financial crisis, the economics of the entertainment industry changed. An insider told me that cruise ships were laying off guest entertainers.

  But by then I'd also come to realize that my spirit craves variety and life as a ship's entertainer wasn't for me, and I gave up on the idea. Money wasted? Perhaps—but I prefer to think it was wisely invested in my own self-discovery. Sour grapes? Maybe—but it's a fact that many projects die on the vine. How would you like to have a job where each time you made money, a proportion, sometimes all, had to be invested in a gamble on the next creative project? I'll admit, over time the process gets somewhat easier. Mistakes help you understand the territory, and you do get smarter about investing your energies.

- ***What about time off?*** Ha-ha. Creativity is never on holiday. Once you get habituated to hustling for each dollar and especially if you have a family to support, your mind becomes attuned to putting food on the table. Creative ideas are your stock-in-trade and the flow never ends. I call it the beautiful curse. Creativity is life, but it also means the work never stops.

  Also, *touring is not a holiday.* I once spent three weeks performing in sunny Australia and got about ninety minutes of beach time. The rest was spent in the day-to-day business of finding food, getting to places, doing online business communication and show preparation.
- ***What about product sales?*** Stuff doesn't sell itself. The marketplace—these days that pretty much means the Internet—is full of jostling competitors. You don't sell a thing without putting time, energy and money into having good stuff and marketing it well. This opens another Pandora's box of dos and don'ts. Suffice it to say you need to be a jack-of-many-trades in order to be master of one. And it's not getting better. My teenage daughter tells me that of all her friends, not one pays for the music they listen to. That's how it is, folks.

Basically I'm saying that becoming a professional performer is a lot less fun behind the curtain than in front. You probably shouldn't do it unless, like me, you have no choice. I have to believe in myself. Even though I'm at an age when many performers are winding down (or at least regurgitating) their former careers, I still have much to do and far to go.

In times when creativity is so culturally undervalued, the only means I know of to continue my work is to appeal to those who understand the struggle of the creative life. So thank you for continuing to support all artists by attending performances and buying our recordings and other merchandise. At the height of World War II it was suggested to Britain's prime minister, Winston Churchill, that funding for the arts be cut in order to support the war effort. Churchill responded, "Then what would we be fighting for?"

The intuitive mind is a sacred gift and the rational mind is a faithful servant. We have created a society that honours the servant and has forgotten the gift.

ALBERT EINSTEIN

CHRISTMAS IN A YORKSHIRE VILLAGE

Think about putting more magic into your performances.

IT'S SNOWING AS I write this. Snow always takes me back to winters and Christmases in the village in the valley where I grew up. As children, the first signs of snow would find us yanking our sleds from sheds and attics where metal runners had been rusting for eight months of the year. We'd hurry up the hill (every direction was uphill from the village), leaving a trail of rust streaks behind us in the snow. Near to one of our favourite slopes lived Monica Ward, a teacher from the village school. Her house stood next to a small grouping of three-hundred-year-old farm buildings.

Monica Ward made real magic one long-ago December day. The ingredients were simple: a woman, a baby, some dress-up clothes and a barn. These, plus some imagination, a little coordination, a bit of nerve and a girl with a star on a stick (who in later life became a singer) were all that was needed to stir deep emotional feelings in the teachers, the children and a loquacious farm woman brought to her spiritual knees, compelled to surrender her ego by the scene she'd helped to create. It was theatre at its finest.

As musicians we should never forget this aspect of what we do. There is so much more to performing than just getting up and singing some songs. What else can you add? Think about it. Allow ideas to come. Act on them. Find whatever ways you can to create magic for the people around you. Sometimes the magic is preplanned, at other times a spontaneous creation, most often a combination of both. But you have to grab it from wherever it comes, shape it into a pleasing form and cast it out towards the senses of your audience. As entertainers we have the opportunity to live at the sharp end of the wand where reality and mystery touch.

Think about making some magic happen. It really does make life worth living. Here's what Monica did.

The approach of Christmas was a time of high spirits in the school. The smell inside each classroom was of glue and poster paint as decorative creations came to life made from glitter, crêpe paper, cotton wool, pine cones and twigs. Those not involved in the making of festive adornments were rehearsing for the school play. Each class did a different play every year, usually written by the teachers themselves.

It was on such a day, probably 1977 or 1978, while Christmas activity was in full swing, when a curious thing happened. Monica Ward dressed up a girl called Frances in a headscarf and robe and sent her off, holding a star on a stick, to deliver a message to every classroom. Frances announced, "Do not be afraid. I bring you good tidings. Follow the star." She beckoned everyone to follow her and each class emptied out towards the playground, where more classes of teachers and pupils waited, mystified.

And so it happened. No permission slips were signed, classroom doors were left open, and everyone in the school just walked away. Everyone, that is, except for Mr. Wainwright, the headmaster. Like the others he was bursting with curiosity, but felt unable to abandon his school. The procession went across the main road, past the post office and down Birks Avenue to where the fields begin. Once over the humpbacked bridge that crosses the River Don, the throng made their way up the hill, turning left at the milk-churn stand to arrive at Whittakers' farm. Curiosity was running high as everyone came to a stop outside a small stone barn. "Why are we here?"

Monica Ward stood in front of the assembled company saying, "We're going to go inside the barn in groups. And when it's your turn to go in, you need to be calm and quiet. Does everybody understand?"

"Yes, miss," came the singsong reply from sixty or so little voices.

Inside the barn it was dark and cobwebby. As the children entered, they were greeted by farm owner Brenda Whittaker. Normally she was a person who revelled in being loud and opinionated, but was now dramatically transformed. In Monica's words Brenda had become "all holy and quiet." Through the gloom the children could make out some bales of hay, and there, in the corner, clothed in a blue gown, was Mary with the baby Jesus.

In truth her name was Caroline, a young woman who had recently given birth to a baby boy. But her baby was now, to all intents and purposes, the baby Jesus. Monica Ward was not a religious woman, but she did feel that some essence of Christmas was becoming lost in the frenzy of eating, drinking and gift giving. She wanted the children to discover a more profound meaning of Christmas—a simple message about a baby being born. She succeeded mightily.

The children stood in awe, gazing at the real Nativity scene before them—a rare moment in life to witness the silent drama of perfect peace. In the cold and quiet of the barn they sang some carols. When Monica describes the atmosphere in the barn that day, she unabashedly calls it *holy.*

Back at school Mr. Wainwright waited, wondering what had happened and where everyone had gone. Soon his teachers and pupils returned to him, safe and unharmed.

ANDA-ONE ANDA-TWO ANDA ONE TWO THREE...

Counting a song in may be harder than you think. It's another musical skill that needs to be learned and practised.

As December ends and we count down the seconds into next year, we forget the time we had to practise counting backwards until we could do it easily. Counting in a song is a similar sort of skill, appearing quite effortless—once you can do it, that is.

If you haven't practised the act of counting in, then it comes as a shock when you're suddenly called on to do it—as happened to me many years ago. I was in my first band, had just introduced a new song to the group, and everyone looked to me to start the music. Standing there holding my banjo I said, "What?"

"Aren't you going to count us in?" they replied.

I had no idea what to do. So it was time for my first lesson in counting in. It was also slightly embarrassing to interrupt a rehearsal so my bandmates could teach me such a basic musical skill. Learning how to deliver a count-in before you're actually required to do it demonstrates a degree of professionalism and confidence. But first we need to ask ourselves the following question:

WHY DO A COUNT-IN?

The count-in achieves two important tasks: (1) it tells all players the exact start of the song; and (2) it communicates the tempo of the song (how fast the song will be played).

If you only ever play alone or if your group doesn't mind sloppy beginnings to songs, then you don't need to count in. Another way to avoid a count-in is to begin every song by playing the last few notes of the melody—like the church organists of my childhood, who would always play the last line of the song so the choir knew when to start singing. But this is not recommended. For example, in rehearsals you may need to count in from the middle of a song.

THE TWO PARTS OF A COUNT-IN

- ***Part 1. Decide on the correct tempo.*** This requires that you get into the head space of the song you're about to play. Take a moment to silently sing a bit of the song in your mind with the feeling you want it to have. (This is often what is going on in the heads of singers whom you see taking a mental pause between songs.) Avoid rushing straight into the next song, or you may start playing at the same tempo as the last song you played. Once you feel you know the tempo of the song, some part of you—an arm, a foot or your head—may move in time to the music you're about to play. This is a way of capturing the tempo in your body as your mind concentrates on the next part of the task.

- ***Part 2. Know which beat the song begins on.*** This is a little tricky at first, but it does get easier. The reason for its trickiness is that counting in a song would be easy if all songs started on the same beat. But they don't. Songs can start on the first, second, third or fourth beats. Here are some examples, all in 4/4 time.

  A song that starts on the *one* beat is "Blue Skies," by Irving Berlin. To count this in, you just need to count to four and the word "Blue" lands on the next *one* beat:

  One-two-three-four: Blue skies / Smiling at me / Nothing but...

  The word "You" from "You Are My Sunshine" happens to come on the *two* beat. The word "sunshine" starts on the *one* beat of the next measure. So you count it in like this:

  One-two-three-four-one: You are my sunshine, my only...

  The Gershwin/Heyward song "Summertime" starts on the *three* beat, so you count it in like this:

  One-two-three-four-one-two: Summertime, and the livin' is easy...

  The song "Tonight You Belong to Me" (as played by Lyle Ritz in *The Jerk*) begins on the *four* beat with the word *I* (from "I know"). The next word, *know*, lands on the next *one* beat. So the count-in goes like this:

  One-two-three-four-one-two-three: I know you belong to somebody new...

Practise by going through your song repertoire and counting in each song. At first you really have to think about it. Eventually you won't need to concentrate so hard and it will become as easy as tying laces, riding a bike and strumming an A-minor-7 chord.

The count-in can be delivered in many forms. In rock bands the drummer sets the pace by clacking his sticks. When studio musicians get intimately familiar with the process, the count-in gets reduced to small bobs of the head followed by an intake of breath.

And when New Year's Eve comes and people are about to do the final countdown of the year, notice how they introduce it. The person leading the countdown often makes sure that everyone starts on time and in the right tempo *by counting in the countdown. Twelve, eleven*... and then everyone is set to come in together on *ten,* and before you know it it's next year and we get to do it all over again.

Four

LEARN FROM THE GREATS

FIVE WAYS TO BECOME A UKULELE GENIUS

Where we learn what genius is and how to develop it, taking our cue from Mozart and the Beatles.

GENIUS IS SOMETHING we're born with, right? How else could Einstein, a simple clerk in a patent office, have changed our world view with his visionary insights? What else could have enabled Mozart to write his first pieces of music at such a young age? (Two years old? C'mon, seriously?) The young Tiger Woods's innate genius for the game was frequently used to explain the almost supernatural way he roared onto the pro-golf scene and tore apart his more experienced opposition.

But what is genius? Those who have studied it have no doubt found many interesting things, but it's what they haven't found out that is most notable. So far researchers have been unable to find a set of brain characteristics that conclusively show the owner of a given brain to be another Einstein, Mozart or Woods.

Our brains develop from birth and change according to environment and activity. Thus the brains of taxi drivers, history teachers and air traffic controllers all end up exhibiting their own special characteristics. But the defining qualities that signify genius are still mostly speculation at this point.

One thing researchers do know is that every acclaimed genius has put in an extraordinary amount of work. At least 10,000 hours and some suggest up to 50,000 hours of dedicated practice. To put that in perspective, they are saying that every genius you've ever heard of did the equivalent of at least twenty hours of practice per week for a period of ten years to get good enough to be recognized as a genius.

"But hold on a moment," I hear you cry. How was Mozart able to put in 10,000 hours before he was two? Well, here's the thing about Mr. Mozart. He was the product of an extraordinarily gifted teacher—his father. Wolfgang Amadeus's dad created and developed innovative music teaching methods that were used with enormous success on both his son and his daughter. (That young Wolfgang became the big success and his sister didn't is partly due to the small matter of gender—girls didn't become music stars in those days. And by the way, if you think our culture has grown beyond such attitudes: quick, right now, name me three *female* geniuses. Because of our social conditioning, that's not quite so easy to do.)

Nowadays, thanks to clever teaching methods, we are used to the sight of six- and seven-year-old violin and piano prodigies. Mozart was not much different from today's Suzuki school graduates, except that he happened to be doing it a few hundred years earlier. "But wait," I hear you cry. "He *wrote music* when he was two!"

Have you heard the music he wrote as a toddler? Has anyone listened to it lately? No, they haven't. And do you know why they haven't? Because it was crap, that's why. Mozart's first major success was at the age of twenty-one, and it was his 271st composition. Before that his education followed a trajectory much like anyone else's. First he copied other composers, and then slowly introduced original concepts into his work as he diligently refined and improved his art.

When the Beatles landed on American shores, they seemed to come out of nowhere. In truth they'd spent years honing their skills, both individually and as a group, performing for eight hours a day, often seven days a week (sometimes even eight days a week—ha-ha) for months on end in some of Hamburg's dingiest nightclubs. In the process they covered countless songs and cultivated their songwriting technique to an extremely high level (see page 168). When the "Fab Four" burst onto the public scene, it was no accident that their chops were tight and their confidence ran high.

Of course, the total amount of time spent working is not the only key to success. I'm sure that if most of us had been opera school classmates of Pavarotti, we might have soon felt discouraged. Pavarotti's talent would have taken him more quickly to a place that we, lesser divas and divos, found unattainable no matter how many hours of ear-bending, glass-breaking fa-sol-la-ti-ing we put in. Nevertheless, my drift is yours for the getting.

If the greatest musical talents had to practise for the equivalent of a shrew's lifetime (about 10,000 hours) to reach their potential, what makes us ukulele players think it's enough to strum for half an hour every three days? Sadly, at least for those of us who took up ukulele believing it was an easy option, the only conclusion to be drawn is this: If you want to be a good ukulele player, you need to practise.

So what can we do to make sure we put in as many ukulele playing hours as possible? Here are five suggestions:

1. ***Practise daily at the same time each day.*** Make your ukulele practice a part of your everyday routine, like brushing your teeth in the morning and answering telemarketing calls at dinnertime. This makes your practice period easier to remember and less easy to skip.
2. ***Find a length of time that works for you.*** Set a timer. Knowing that you have a fixed amount of time available to practise can help you use that time to the fullest. Even if it is short, aim to maximize whatever time you've set aside for yourself.
3. ***Practise often.*** Sometimes life doesn't permit us to take longer breaks, so play when you can. Say, between tasks or seeing clients. Ten lots of three-minute practice sessions is the same as one half-hour session. If you take your ukulele to work, this tip will be useful for all you taxi drivers and air traffic controllers. No planes coming in right now? Strum a few bars of a song by Lady Gaga.
4. ***Perform and jam as often as possible with as many people as you can.*** Playing live adds a layer of intensity that helps the mind to focus. Much learning comes from playing for and with others.
5. ***Reward yourself.*** The work will be so much more bearable if you know there will be a movie, a pleasant beverage or a banana coming to you at the end of it.

There. I've finished. Now for that banana. Mmm, mm, that's good. It's hungry work being a genius.

LONGEVITY TIPS FROM THE WORLD'S OLDEST UKULELE ENTERTAINER

Here I share some things I learned from the long career of Bill Tapia.

BILL TAPIA PASSED away peacefully on December 2, 2011, aged 103 years. His incredible professional career spanned more than ninety years. At ten years old he was already playing "The Stars and Stripes Forever" on his ukulele at shows for the World War I troops. Amazingly, he'd learned the song directly from the composer, after hearing it played by John Philip Sousa's own band. By age twelve he was playing in vaudeville. He later moved on to play guitar as a jazz sideman. He had many notable highlights, including occasions when he got to accompany Louis Armstrong, Elvis Presley, Billie Holiday and Bing Crosby. It's even said that he was the one to introduce legendary broadcaster Arthur Godfrey to the ukulele.

Towards the end of his life the remarkable centenarian was touring again, performing live shows, recording CDs and signing them for countless fans of all ages. He is said to have been the oldest unionized performing musician ever.

Words like "remarkable," "amazing" and "incredible" come easily to mind when thinking about Bill Tapia. Such superlatives arise from a rare combination: his spritely old age plus his renowned talent as an entertainer. In a world where much of our music gets generated by the young, it can feel both surreal and slightly overwhelming to contemplate the human scale of time that was travelled by Mr. Tapia and his uke.

As for me, I already feel old. I bruise more easily and my joints don't bend with the flexibility that they did in my younger days. That was back when I was said to be the spitting image of Michelangelo's "David" (well, one person said it anyway). I've also had my share of root canals, strained ligaments and grey hairs. My eyesight is pretty good but it's clear to see that it's not everything it was. I'm not complaining, but here's what really gets me: to reach Bill Tapia's final resting age, I will have to live my whole life again and then several years on top of that. And quite frankly I find it hard to imagine.

To gain some perspective on the length of his career, consider this: when Bill Tapia was a little boy there were no cars, radios or refrigerators. Or if there were, *he* wasn't aware of them. As a young Hawaiian boy in 1915 he bought his first uke from Manuel Nunes, inventor of the ukulele, for 75 cents. He was already strumming ukulele chords when the instrument was only just being introduced to the United States mainland. The roaring twenties hadn't even started.

We now think of Hapa Haole music, that is, non-indigenous Hawaiian songs like "Ukulele Lady," "My Little Grass Shack" and "Sweet Leilani," popularized in the 1920s and '30s, as being positively archaic. Bill Tapia was playing those songs when they first came out and could only be heard either live or issuing from the sound cones of wind-up gramophones. And he was hearing and playing jazz right when jazz was invented. It's nothing short of astounding.

Shortly before Bill Tapia's one hundredth birthday, he and I performed in the main concert at the Southern California Ukulele Festival in Cerritos, California. We'd both completed our sets and, as musicians often do, we were watching the rest of the show while standing near the back of the concert hall.

The thought occurred to me that this was a unique opportunity to speak with Bill. Perhaps I could glean some secrets that might help me survive the rigours of musicianship for as long as he had done. I said, "I want to be doing this when I'm ninety-nine. Do you have any hints or advice to pass on?" He thought for a moment and then answered me in four words. "Just keep doing it."

I almost left it at that, but then decided to push the matter a little further. I said, "No, come on, Bill, there's got to be more to it." He thought for a spell and said, "Well, I always took pretty good care of myself. I didn't take drugs and I wasn't a drinker except for a social drink. I exercised by riding my bike every day until my doctor said I had to stop because of angina, but even now I walk daily. The only bad thing I did was to smoke two packs of cigarettes a day until I was eighty-seven. I quit smoking because of the angina."

Here then, as far as I can surmise, are Bill Tapia's seven rules for a long and healthy musical life.

LONG LIFE RULE #1 Have the good fortune to be born with long-life genes.

LONG LIFE RULE #2 Be born into a time when everyone eats natural organic food and there are no unhealthy petroleum or corn-derived products. Neither is there electromagnetic radiation from cellphone towers, nuclear power stations, radio transmitters or X-rays. (There could still be the occasional world war or flu epidemic to survive, but hopefully, with luck and some help from number one, you'll sail through all those.)

LONG LIFE RULE #3 Exercise daily.

LONG LIFE RULE #4 Don't do drugs and only drink alcohol in moderation.

LONG LIFE RULE #5 If you smoke heavily it's a good idea to quit, at least by the time you're in your late eighties.

LONG LIFE RULE #6 Play ukulele and sing.

LONG LIFE RULE #7 Just keep doing it.

CREATING THE NON-EXISTENT

Becoming the performer you want to be is a journey of exploration. Let's look at what it takes to get there.

LISTENING RECENTLY TO an entrepreneur talk about how he started his business, I was struck by his wording. He said, "Since the type of company I was looking for could not be found in the world, I reasoned that I would have to create something that doesn't presently exist."

Those words are also apt when it comes to the creation and development of a captivating performance persona.

Great performers appear to have it easy. When they get onstage it seems they can do no wrong. The way they look, move, talk, sing, etc. are all parts of a unique wholeness: a complete vision of what we have come to expect them to be. We wonder how they got to be that way and imagine that their character came about by some lucky fluke of birth, or perhaps in a single blinding flash of realization. In truth, such performers develop their public personalities both consciously and incrementally.

The first instinct for most of us, once we've decided we are going to perform for others, is to emulate musicians we admire. We soon realize, however, that the full-scale copying of someone else's act, unless you're a tribute band, is both highly work-intensive and self-defeating. We need to find for ourselves a combination of onstage character traits that will lead people to describe us as one-of-a-kind, captivating, electrifying, funny, moving, engaging, delightful, and so on.

Developing your onstage persona is an ongoing process of experimentation. As someone looking to have a more engaging stage presence, you need to be constantly on the hunt for new ideas. Such ideas may come from your own experience or from watching others. They may pop into your mind unexpectedly or they may be a result of fortuitous accident.

Since there is no blueprint for creating the non-existent, I was, at this point in my narrative, about to give you particular examples of discoveries and innovations some performers made that drastically changed how they were perceived by an audience. It then struck me that one of the most memorable entertainment figures ever created was a certain Mr. Tiny Tim: a singular individual who rose to fame in the late 1960s. Whether you loved him or hated him, you never forgot him. What I find most interesting is not just the fact that he manufactured his image piece by piece until he'd achieved mass public exposure, but that he was also a highly self-absorbed individual who loved to talk about his life and his process.

In the book *Tiny Tim*, by Harry Stein, Tiny says, "After Jesus took over I stopped worrying. I'd been a constant worrier, but now I just placed myself in his hands. I prayed about my career, and one morning, like a revelation, I woke up and had the answer. It came to me like that, through prayer: I would use a high voice."

Tiny goes on to relate how his new voice felt natural and original. So much so "I even made myself swoon," he says.

But although his own soul was nourished by this discovery, the same can't be said for his immediate family, especially his father, who had been one of the few to like Tiny's original voice and who now thought he sounded like a sissy. But Tiny reasoned that since he was far from good-looking, this new voice might be the answer he'd been seeking. The style sounded the way he looked. And he knew from his knowledge of crooners like Rudy Vallée and Frank Sinatra that critics were always harsh when a new voice came on the scene. Proof of this wisdom came when he tried the new voice at a talent show at the Old Alliance Club in St. Mark's Place. After singing "You Are My Sunshine" he says, "I couldn't believe how the audience responded. As I sang, a cry of amazement swept the room, like a hundred people saying, 'Oooooh!' Then they started shouting and laughing, and when I came back for applause, they gave me a big ovation."

Whether or not you agree with Tiny Tim's often hypocritical religious beliefs, you have to admire his courageous devotion in creating for himself a persona that was so unique. Even his stage name, Tiny Tim, was a result of trial and error, following less memorable monikers such as Larry Love and Darry Dove. The freak show combination of his long hair, slightly grotesque features, eye-catching suits, makeup and falsetto voice formed a character so captivating that his signature image and voice became known throughout the world.

And there was something else about him too, something which at the time was both weird and innovative. Now what was it? Oh yes, he played a ukulele. Now, imagine that!

ANVIL AND THE FAMILY IN THE PARK

A documentary film and a bicycle ride make me consider a key lesson for all of us who struggle with our art and performance.

THE MOST DEPRESSING part of this story was the bike ride. So let's get that over with first. It was a beautiful autumn day and people were dressed warmly as they played, strolled and kicked at leaves in the park. As long as you were in the sunshine it wasn't a cold day—quite pleasant, in fact. And on entering the park I slowed my pace to enjoy the sight of people communing with the outdoors in countless different ways.

My eye was caught by a small boy, about three years old, who was about to kick a soccer ball to his father. The ball seemed half as big as the boy and I wondered how he'd manage. The boy ran at the ball. His kick connected far better than I ever thought it could. He shouted with joy, and I looked at the father's face to watch his response. Instead of taking delight in his son's achievement, he was deeply engrossed in a phone conversation and paying only cursory attention to his son. The boy, however, continued to kick the ball surprisingly well, while shouting enthusiastically to his mentally absent dad.

Meanwhile the boy's mother was filming this activity. Her camera followed the two of them as the husband trailed after his son at a pace slow enough to ensure that he wouldn't catch up with the boy and thereby have to interrupt his call. It broke my heart to see the boy's exuberant enthusiasm on display while his parents remained completely disengaged.

I don't own a mobile phone and therefore have no temptation to talk, text and take pictures during every waking moment. This is perhaps why I'm so appalled at the increasing disengagement of people from the present. My mind fast-forwarded to a time when the boy's unbridled enthusiasm might suddenly halt as he looked around and realized that his efforts were going unnoticed and unappreciated, that others were too engaged in their hand-held communication devices to spare any attention for him. I wondered, what will happen then? Will he try harder? Or will he eventually quit the wearisome effort of showing how great life can be and, in turn, curl up in his own technological cocoon? As I said, it was a depressing moment, but quickly alleviated by remembering the life-affirming message in the movie *Anvil! The Story of Anvil.*

The band Anvil, a heavy-metal combo formed in Toronto in 1978, teetered on the brink of fame when they co-headlined Japan's Super Rock festival in 1984. The other headliners were the Scorpions, Whitesnake and Bon Jovi. All these bands went on to sell millions of records while Anvil—whose name literally means a big lump of heavy metal—sank into obscurity.

The 2008 film catches up with Anvil thirty years from their formation. Steve "Lips" Kudlow, on lead vocal and lead guitar, now drives a truck for Children's Choice Catering, which delivers children's meals to schools and institutions. He reflects on why the band, after thirty years and twelve albums, has still made no headway in becoming successful. The film follows them on a European tour where everything goes wrong. They get lost, miss trains, don't get paid, and when they finally get to Transylvania to play the Monsters of Rock festival in a 10,000-seat arena, only 174 people show up. From such a description you might think the movie would be a dreary, or at least a farcical, bad-luck story, but not so. Part of its charm is the brilliant filmmaking of Sacha Gervasi (Anvil fan and former Anvil roadie), but what really grabbed me was the tireless optimism of "Lips" himself. There are many moments in the film where he is dealt severe setbacks, and we see him momentarily mourn his ill fortune. And then, again and again, we watch his spirit rebuild by sheer dint of his own personal optimism. Seeing him transform his outlook over and over like this we come to realize what has made him, and his close friend, drummer Robb Reiner, hang in for all these years.

I say life is worth nothing if we don't try to make our dreams come true, and "Lips" Kudlow understands this concept instinctively. All musicians, artists and performers understand the power of holding on to a dream—even when things get dire. Sometimes misfortune can take place over a period of years—as in Anvil's case—or the misery may be agonizingly brief, such as when we perform a disastrous show for an unappreciative crowd. That sort of show can leave you questioning both your purpose and your commitment.

Longevity has its own value. There is majesty in not giving up. Going through the personal fires of soul-searing performance agony and coming out the other side really does make us better in so many more ways than just as entertainers. It gives us empathy for the myriad struggles of others and helps us understand what things in life are truly important—and which aren't.

The wonderful irony of the film is that its popularity has made Anvil a cult phenomenon, finally giving them a measure of fame that includes (paid) concert bookings all over the world.

As the years go by, I'll wonder about that little boy and his talent and enthusiasm for kicking a ball. I pray that, regardless of whether people notice him, he will never give up. May he always delight in the physicality of playing outdoors. And as he grows I want him to keep striving to shoot farther, higher and ever more gracefully. Perhaps he'll even reach a goal at some point—but truthfully, I really don't think that matters too much.

HOW TO BE A GREAT MUSIC TEACHER PART I: HAVE FUN

J. Chalmers Doane was the four-string evangelist who got thousands of Canadian kids playing D-tuned ukulele in the 1960s and 1970s. His much wider goal was to transmit the love of music to as many people as possible.

FOR THOSE OF us who played ukulele before about 1995, there were few heroes to draw from. The Internet was still very new then, so any ukulele heroes we did have were known because of their presence in movies, recordings and TV. Names like Tiny Tim, George Formby, Lyle Ritz, Roy Smeck, Arthur Godfrey. And the Hawaiian scene was pretty much unavailable except to the comparatively few who actually went there. But as I hunted libraries and thrift stores for tidbits of ukulele knowledge, another name kept surfacing: J. Chalmers Doane.

His name is legendary in Canada (among uke players at least) as the man who in the 1960s had the brilliant idea of teaching ukulele to children by bringing the instrument to hundreds of schools across Canada. In fact, it was his *Ukulele in the Classroom* method that I kept seeing in music stores. A collector friend once gave me a copy of that book. It was signed on the front: *To Arthur Godfrey. Best Wishes from Chalmers Doane.*

I returned this artifact to Chalmers while attending Nova Scotia's Ukulele Ceilidh in 2009. Since then, while at BC's annual Langley Ukulele Workshop, I've been fortunate to teach with Chalmers as well as two more brilliant descendants of his work: Peter Luongo and James Hill. That I, a self-taught player, should get to teach alongside these gifted and trained teachers is, in itself, strangely unreal to me. And the fact that I'm there at all is thanks to James Hill, who I presume feels I have something to offer ukulele students that is outside the scope of traditional music teaching. Whatever his reasons, I'm grateful and indebted to him for giving me the chance to know J. Chalmers Doane.

Seeing his name on so many dusty old music books gave me the impression that the writer, if still alive, was probably clinging to life by a thread and having his dinner served through a straw. It was amazing to discover that the almost mythical J. Chalmers Doane was not only very much alive, but extremely healthy and energetic. I also found him to have a childlike mind for inventiveness and play. This surprised me because his *Ukulele in the Classroom* method—essentially a manual for learning the basics of music via the ukulele—was stuffed with scales and basic melodies that to me seemed at odds with the type of enjoyment I was getting from the instrument. So I expected him to be a staid schoolteacherly type. That idea of him changed once I'd made him laugh.

Not everyone gets my sense of humour. I like to amuse people, but I couldn't tell you why my brain sometimes makes the leaps and connections that it does. Often what comes out of my mouth isn't a joke in the standard sense, but rather a twisted way of looking at a situation that leaves it up to the listener to figure out the rest. Somehow, for whatever reason, Chalmers and I are a good fit. He likes my sense of the ridiculous, and I adore his snapshots-of-life stories that flash brilliantly with playful inventiveness, a love of excellence and a care for people. One October I took him up on his offer to visit his home in Nova Scotia.

"He was twenty-eight when he became head of Halifax's school music program," his wife Jean was telling me over a cup of tea in her kitchen. "He worked hard," she continued, "but he made it a rule to have fun every day."

I don't remember exactly where Chalmers was at the time Jean said this—he might have been keeping a tennis appointment with friends who regularly meet to battle it out on his home-made tennis court. As Chalmers toured me around the house, sheds and fields that comprise his property, I learned about other ways that he has fun in his life. He has a home-made Sjoelbak game (Dutch shuffleboard) in the living room, a ping-pong table in the basement, a pool table in an old barn, and outside on a sloping field there's a home-made six-hole golf course that has never seen the care of a professional greensman but does the job quite adequately.

After dinner the games began. First I lost at Sjoelbak. Then out to the barn, where he thrashed me eight games to one at pool. By then we were warmed up for the slightly more strenuous exertions of basement ping-pong. In half a dozen games I didn't even come close. The guy is the same age as my mom. Such a losing streak might have been embarrassing had not the evening been so enjoyable.

As we sat in his living room, exhausted (at least I was) from our evening's jousting, Chalmers innocently asked me, "What do you do for fun at home in Vancouver?"

And with that question he had me. I was stumped, flummoxed and at a complete loss. My gut instinct told me that having a beer in front of the TV didn't count; reading didn't count; cycling, jogging and other exercise probably didn't count—unless they included an element of socializing—which for me they don't; solo ukulele practice didn't count since it's been my occupation for two decades. In that moment I realized that *play* time and fun are vital qualifications you need to have in order to pass a full and balanced life. Chalmers assured me I was fine, but I felt I was failing somehow.

As you read this, do you think you have enough fun in your life? I know that residing in a downtown apartment, as I do, isn't exactly conducive to creating a golf course. But there's a nice pitch-and-putt over at the park, there's a community centre with ping-pong, skating, badminton and a host of other activities (all previously disdained by me as the domain of people with nothing better to do). I've now learned—thanks to Chalmers—that it's time to look at play in a new light.

HOW TO BE A GREAT MUSIC TEACHER PART 2: THINK LATERALLY

Playful fun is a guiding consciousness that made J. Chalmers Doane into a legendary educator. Here's how that worked.

IT'S ASTOUNDING TO realize that Canadian high-school teachers have to play and teach every single instrument in their high-school bands. And Chalmers was no exception. To this day he can pick up and play any one of a dozen or so instruments. Jam with him at a festival and he's more likely to play clarinet or double bass than ukulele. Think about that for a moment. His uke is in D tuning, his clarinet in B-flat, and the bass is in, well, whatever basses are tuned in. None of that matters to Chalmers. In fact, he finds the discussion over which ukulele tuning is the superior one, C or D, to be completely irrelevant. You may find this surprising, since it's because of his use of D-tuned ukulele that kids across Canada still learn on D-tuned instruments.

And believe me, at the Langley Ukulele Workshop, debates regarding C or D superiority have been known to get a little heated. But Chalmers says that so long as you're playing the right note or chord, it matters not whether you're in C tuning, D tuning, strumming a balalaika or blowing bagpipes. End of discussion. You'll actually get far more passion out of him if you should happen to ask him how to *practise.*

I've seen Chalmers talk for fifteen minutes on the subject of what *real* music practice is. His thesis essentially boils down to making practice fun. If you're going to be playing the same thing over and over again, find ways to make it entertaining for yourself so that it stays fresh and interesting. That notion of entertainment is the key to Chalmers' phenomenal success as an educator.

At one period in his life he taught adult marching bands. The outdoor practices occurred near a military training base, where at particular times on certain days the army would do parachute jumps. Chalmers noted these times so that when he was out with a new group of players he'd tell them, "We're going to start playing now, but in two minutes you're going to see a plane fly overhead and a guy is going to jump out just over there."

Imagine the momentary thrill those new musicians got when his prophecy came true. That sense of wonder is something we normally associate with movies. But it takes a mind like Chalmers' to bring magic to life, and his particular genius was to connect that feeling to making music. Basically Chalmers is a fiendishly clever trickster, somewhat like Brer Rabbit, Tom Sawyer and Bart Simpson all rolled into one. But he's different in the sense that his evolved form of trickery only results in mutually beneficial outcomes. That is, win-win situations.

Here's one example. He once owned a wood-splitting machine, with which he'd cut wood for his winter heating. Noticing that his neighbour, a somewhat younger fellow, was cutting his wood laboriously by hand, Chalmers got to thinking. Eventually they struck a deal whereupon he gave away his wood splitter to the neighbour, who in return promised to cut Chalmers' firewood for as long as they remained neighbours. It was a clever little deal that both parties are still delighted with.

A classroom story that I really enjoyed was one where he asked the kids to listen really hard to a short piece of music in which, at some moment, a triangle would sound. On hearing the triangle he told them they should raise their hands. But then, just at the moment the triangle was played, Chalmers had a loud and sudden coughing fit. At the end of the piece he asked, "Who heard the triangle?" No one had. "Hmm, that's very strange," he said, "because it was definitely there. I'll play it again. Listen more carefully."

This time when the triangle sounded Chalmers was over by the classroom door and with perfect timing he slammed it shut. Again the piece ended and he asked if anyone had heard the triangle this time. Still no one had. "That is really so peculiar because it's definitely there, clear as a bell. Let's try again." So again the process was repeated, with some other timely distraction. On the fourth time he played the piece—without coughs, bangs or yells—the sound of the triangle rang brightly around the classroom and every hand shot up.

Listening is the first major skill that a musician must acquire, and I have never heard a more brilliant and playful way to get kids to listen over and over again to the same bit of music with full focus and intention. That one lesson was a marvelous education for them. And along with the lesson came a feeling of delight. What child among them could help wondering what the trickster teacher would have in store for them next class?

I believe that what makes J. Chalmers Doane such an Einstein of education is that when he puts his mind to a problem, he refuses to give up until he's found an elegant solution. Most other educators just aren't thinking that way. But it's worth doing. The habit of thinking in novel ways will transport the brain to new and interesting destinations—always useful when making music. And I love this type of lateral thinking.

In the lunchroom at the Langley Ukulele Workshop, some of the uke teachers were eating sandwiches when Jim D'Ville happened to mention a 1964 Buck Owens hit single that had reached number one in the *Billboard* charts. "What happened next was remarkable," he told us, "because the B-side of the same record then took the place of the A-side in the number one spot." This was a unique occurrence in musical history apparently.

I said, "But Jim, my understanding is that records reach their chart position according to record sales." Yes. Jim agreed.

"Well surely," I continued, "it was the same record!"

This simple thought twist tickled Chalmers, and afterwards he mentioned to me that he was entertained by my way of thinking. The next morning the faculty members were together again, this time for brunch and to discuss how the workshop weekend had gone. Once again the discussion of teaching with C- or D-tuned ukuleles came up. And again Chalmers gave his opinion that it doesn't really matter.

I said, "His name is Chalmers Doane, so that can be *C* or *D*." Peter Luongo quickly jumped in, saying, "But it's *J.* Chalmers Doane. What does the *J* stand for?" Eagerly Chalmers responded, "It means *Just* C or D." His face lit up as he turned towards me, saying, "See, I'm getting better at this!"

PUSH AND POLISH, BEATLES STYLE

While recording my albums Love and Laughter, I started musing on what made the most famous recording artists so outstanding.

"IT'S THE ULTIMATE geek book for recording engineers," said producer and guitarist extraordinaire Steve Dawson. I was sitting cross-legged on the studio floor during a break in recording. The whopping tome I'd just opened was holding down the base of a microphone stand, which in turn supported a draped blanket used to acoustically screen my area of the studio from the other musicians. The book contained every bit of known information about how the Beatles recorded their music: technical specifications of studios, instruments, amplifiers and indeed every object ever involved in creating a sound on a Beatles album. It struck me how far the makers of those iconic albums had gone in their quest to make sounds that had previously not existed.

Of course, fame and money help. It's expensive to experiment on a big scale, and 1960s recording companies were investing heavily in all kinds of bands—some of whom were recording works every bit as creative and interesting as what the Beatles were doing: the Beach Boys, Marvin Gaye, the Doors, the Velvet Underground, the Kinks, Frank Zappa and more. But none came close to gaining the exponentially disproportionate fame that the Beatles achieved.

This got me thinking about the elements that drove the Beatles' career to such high levels. My conclusion is that they had a pair of vital attributes I call *push* and *polish,* which they applied to every aspect of their music. I first turned on to this concept while reading an interview with Steve Miller (of the Steve Miller Band). He said that Paul McCartney once advised him to take special care with songwriting—to keep working on a song even when you think it's done. With this in mind, let us compare and contrast ways that a supremely great band differs from the average amateur Joe Maestro.

MUSICIANSHIP

- ***What less effective musicians do:*** They practise their instrument until they get "good enough." At this point their desire to get better dwindles, as they take comfort in the thought that any mistakes they make will be covered up by the others.
- ***What the Beatles did:*** Every member of the band put in thousands of playing hours to get their musical skills up to scratch. In recent years when Beatles master tapes are pulled out of the vaults, engineers can isolate and hear individual instruments. It is very evident that there was no sloppy playing going on. Every member of the group added to the overall sound.

PERFORMANCE

- ***What less effective musicians do:*** They learn some songs and practise them until they sound "good enough." Over time the performance of each song doesn't get any better. In fact, it often worsens because they're no longer consciously working towards improvement.
- ***What the Beatles did:*** They performed in a whorehouse in Hamburg for eight to ten hours a day, six or seven days a week, for months on end. They sought out and studied great songs and learned how to present them with

musicality, energy and style. When lesser performers go to whorehouses, it's usually not to become better musicians.

SONGWRITING

- ***What less effective musicians do:*** Often they'll copy a song they like, but to make it "original" they tweak and change the melody, and end up with something bland and forgettable. Either that or they come up with a brand new melody that just happens to be bland and forgettable, and then don't bother to improve on it. The chord changes either remain identical to standard songs or are so random that they sound weird and unsuitable. Lyrics are jotted down but barely go through any sort of editing process, grammar is confused, clichés abound, and ideas and lyric lines are pedestrian and predictable. But mostly no one can tell because they never learned to sing clearly enough to make their lyrics understandable anyway.
- ***What the Beatles did:*** Every song they wrote was honed and polished. They crafted melodies until they were unique, memorable and singable. They wrote lyrics to express exactly what they wanted to say, and they devised chord changes and harmonies that were surprising and appealing.

RECORDING

- ***What less effective musicians do:*** They connect microphones to a computer and discover that they have exponentially more ways to manipulate sound than the Beatles team ever dreamed possible. Unfortunately, without pushing to take the product to the highest standard possible, they end up with results that sound amateurish. However, this doesn't matter because the creator is still able to proudly say, in a fake Liverpool accent, "Ah've just ricawded me new CD. D'yah fancy a listen?"
- ***What the Beatles did:*** With a lot of help from producer George Martin, they pushed the boundaries of what was possible. Multi-track recording was still in its infancy, but they achieved amazing results (especially when

you consider that the *Sgt. Pepper* album was recorded on a four-track machine). This was done with a team of people (producer, sound engineers and musicians) who had individually studied their craft and who strove together to reach new realms of recording artistry.

Most of us at some time have displayed aspects of lazy creativity—indeed, it's a necessary part of the learning process—but we should remember how the Beatles pushed further and polished finer every aspect of their creativity. Let's bring that same consciousness to our own work.

GEORGE FORMBY (A.K.A. PAUL CASPER)

The tale of how I got to know a very special George Formby re-enactor.

THIS STORY BEGINS and ends in a lovely old English pub with wonky floors and low timbers called The Huntsman. It's in Thurlstone, the same Yorkshire village where Father David got his legs waxed (as heard on my *Laughter* album). I performed in this pub in 2004 and well remember my surprise at suddenly seeing Rod Stewart and Tina Turner in the crowd. They were celebrity look-alikes who happened to live nearby. Also there, though I never noticed him that night, was another look-alike, their nephew Paul Casper.

It was Dave Fields the landlord who introduced me to Paul in 2007. He'd already mentioned a local who bore a resemblance to George Formby, but I didn't pay him too much mind: anyone who has been to a George Formby Society convention will tell you that although many do a good job of sounding like George, none truly look like him. Paul Casper *does* look like him. It's uncanny. Spend some time with Paul and you start to believe he *is* Formby. Everything about him carries an essence of George: the unstoppable smile, a natural humility and a quick, down-to-earth sense of humour. The quality of his vocal inflections is George-like too—so you barely notice that Paul's accent is Yorkshire, unlike Formby's Lancashire (a different accent you can hear by travelling a mere twenty miles west from Thurlstone). We sat down on one of the pub benches while he told me about himself.

Paul had played guitar as a teenage punk rocker but he'd never strummed a ukulele. This was his deliberate choice, since he'd never been happy with his natural resemblance to the ukulele star. But to me it was obvious from our first meeting that he was a sensation just waiting to happen, and I kept insisting that he rethink his position and at least try out a ukulele. Paul was still reluctant, however. After a lifetime of people saying, "Has anyone ever told you, you're just like George Formby?" he wasn't really interested. Even his spiky-haired punk look had not been enough to hide his Formbyesque features. Paul said, "You could have put a gas mask on me and I'd still have looked like him."

Bit by bit his resolve began to crack as I doggedly persisted that he should have a shot at learning some Formby songs. If it didn't work out, I pressed, he could always drop it and be no worse off. In the end we made a pact that by the next time I returned to England, he would try playing a ukulele.

Paul was as good as his word. Two and a half years later I returned to perform at The Huntsman again. This time Paul, now the owner of a banjo ukulele, was able to join me for a couple of Formby songs. It turned out that landlord Dave had given him a cheap Mahalo ukulele and a chord book. Paul was perplexed at first by the high strings on top and bottom, but became delighted by his first few chords. When he joined me at the microphone to sing "Our Sergeant Major" and "My Little Stick of Blackpool Rock," the approving audience made it clear that as George Formby he could do no wrong. Months later when he lost his job (driving forklift in a cold store warehouse), his new career as a ukulele entertainer was already underway.

It's a fabulous irony that his Aunt Nova and Uncle Gerry worked for years in the celebrity look-alike business as Tina Turner and Rod Stewart. They played their parts in encouraging Paul's Formby career and got him his first booking in Southampton, to perform at Sir Norman Wisdom's ninety-first birthday party. (Norman Wisdom, a brilliant British comedian of the Formby era, sat just six feet in front of Paul as he performed his new Formby act. It was a nerve-wracking way to begin, and to this day Paul has never felt so nervous during a performance.)

Paul Casper's *George Formby Experience* has gone from strength to strength. He has performed his show all over the United Kingdom, including at 1940s re-enactments, at numerous World War II veterans shows, and twice at events attended by Queen Elizabeth II. A highlight for him was the Preston Guild Ball in 2012—a show originally scheduled for 1942 but cancelled due to World War II and finally revived exactly seventy years later. On YouTube you can see Paul playing "Leaning on a Lamppost" at that show.

Paul has come to terms with being George Formby. When asked how he feels about playing the part of the 1940s superstar, he philosophically replies, "The way I look at it, everything in life is an act anyway. We're prone to do certain things because we were brought up in a certain way—the way we react and so on. So nothing's real. All the days in our lives are an act. Being Formby just pushes that to a different level."

So it seems that Paul has made peace with his alter ego and now happily signs autographs as *George Formby (a.k.a. Paul Casper).* In November 2013 Paul performed his show to a packed Huntsman pub (celebrating the fourth anniversary of the new landlord) and our story came full circle. "It was phenomenal," Paul said. "I was performing in the place where Ralph was when I first saw him."

It's nice how things turn out. Or, rather, to use Formby's famous catchphrase, "It's turned out nice again!"

A TALE OF TWO UKES

My two near-identical ukuleles were very different in one important respect.

IT WAS THE best of ukes; it was the worst of ukes. During the mid-1990s, the renowned Larrivée Guitars company was making high-end ukuleles for Japan, a market where people were enjoying a ukulele craze so entrenched that ukuleles were even being used to keep rhythm in step-exercise classes. Japan's economy was in high gear, and Larrivée soprano ukuleles were selling for around $2,000 apiece.

I'd sent a copy of my newly released album *King of the Ukulele* to the Larrivée factory in Vancouver and was invited for a meeting with company owner Jean Larrivée and his son John Larrivée Jr. I was delighted when Jean Larrivée Sr. told me he rarely listens to music, but that he'd listened to my CD several times and loved it. His son John nodded his head, saying, "Yeah, he never does that."

Seated in their office, I was surprised when Jean took out a paper bag and dumped its mystifying contents—a vintage Martin ukulele (sawn into several pieces)—onto my lap. It was shocking to think of them deliberately destroying a perfectly good Martin. But, as John told me, "Sacrifices must be made if you want to learn to build a great uke."

Inside the ukulele shop, I was then shown approximately fifteen ukuleles on a workbench and invited to try them out. This was a time when good-quality ukuleles were rare, and the chance to play so many perfectly built little instruments was an unusual privilege. I asked John about how the building process compares to the manufacture of guitars. He replied, "It takes as much work to build a good ukulele as a good guitar, just less wood."

I floated out of there with two ukuleles: a mahogany concert uke and a koa soprano, each with ebony fingerboards and inlaid with abalone and sterling silver. That soprano ukulele got, and still gets, a lot of use. It was the instrument I played on my 2003 DVD *The Complete Ukulele Course*, and to this day it hangs by my desk, always ready to be played.

About six years after I acquired those ukes, I learned that a local pawnbroker and music store was selling a Larrivée soprano for $600. It was in immaculate condition. By then Larrivée had quit making ukuleles. John told me that the ukulele boom in Japan had cooled off, and despite my repeated protests to the contrary, they felt that the high-end ukulele market didn't offer a profitable future. I bought the pawnshop ukulele, figuring $600 for a pristine Larrivée was a fair investment. I could either sell it for a profit or hold on to it in case some calamity befell my present instrument. When I got home I made the jaw-dropping discovery that this new instrument had serial number 32348, whereas my own was 32349. They'd likely been side by side on the ukulele shop bench that day I visited. I put my new Larrivée on a shelf and that's where it remained for several years.

I hardly looked at it again until 2011, when I landed the job of providing ukulele sound-over work for two separate Hollywood movies. In each case the actor was playing ukulele quite adequately but, because of some musicians union issue that was never made clear to me, the moviemakers needed to get the ukulele parts re-recorded outside the country. The uke in one movie was tuned with a high G string and the other with low G. Not having a ukulele with a low G string, I retrieved my spare Larrivée from the shelf, restrung it for low G and proceeded to play. That's when I realized something was very wrong.

My initial reaction was denial. It didn't seem plausible for a Larrivée ukulele to sound so profoundly bad. But my ears did not deceive me: the intonation was off, but not just a bit off (like a badly made cheap uke), it was *way* off. I looked at both instruments from every angle, and only when I held them face to face did I discover that the bridge on the new one was about 1 centimetre closer to the sound hole than the bridge on my original uke.

My wife Kathryn was incensed that I'd been ripped off by the geographically misnomered San Francisco Pawnbrokers. Her reaction was futile, however, since the store had closed down some years before. And her anger was contrasted by my own feeling of quiet delight at being the owner of a rare bird, that is, a renegade Larrivée that had cunningly gotten through quality control unchecked. Over time my joy in owning a collectible mistake (akin perhaps to finding a postage stamp with the queen's head printed upside down) was replaced with the annoyance of owning an unplayable instrument, inflamed with chagrin, as I realized my wife was once again right.

And so, in March 2014, while visiting the local music shop West Coast Guitars, I told my story to owners Glen and Shannon. While looking at my original ukulele and its unplayable twin, Glen had a compelling notion. He suggested that if the bridge on the bad uke were unglued, turned around the other way and glued back down in the same location, this would place the saddle towards the back of the bridge (exactly at the point where it needed to be) and incur no tell-tale mark on the front of the instrument showing that the bridge had been moved. We both thought this was a splendid idea. Unfortunately, his luthier didn't agree, citing the lack of space for the necessary string slots: a vital feature.

And so, it is a far far better thing that I do. I have asked a luthier to move the bridge. Sure, there'll now be a mark on the face of the ukulele, divulging the instrument's imperfect past. And I'll forfeit the cachet of owning the ukulele equivalent of a misprinted sheet of Penny Black stamps (should there be any future trade in misbuilt ukuleles). But at least my instrument will now be playable, and after all, isn't that the most important thing?

Postscript: After writing the above piece, I ran into John Larrivee Jr. and told him the tale. He doesn't believe the ukulele would ever have left the factory without him knowing the problem. He thinks the most likely explanation is that it got stolen from the discard bin and pawned by a past employee looking to make a bit of money on the side.

CHECK OUT THIS NEW PERFORMER!

By taking a look at the skills of an extraordinary showman, we discover eight new ways we can enrich our own shows.

I GENERALLY DON'T WRITE much about other performers. That's not really surprising, since most entertainers feel it prudent and profitable to promote themselves at every opportunity—while mentioning the work of others as little as possible. The typical performer's attitude in this musical rat race is, "I work hard to get noticed. The others can darn well find their own publicity."

If I've written about other entertainers at all, it is generally because their fame and longevity has put their work in such a different category from my own that they don't pose a threat to my lofty career goals. Examples of these include firmly established icons such as Lyle Ritz and Chalmers Doane or the equally iconic names of George Formby, Bill Tapia and May Singhi Breen, who are perhaps even more firmly established—and non-threatening by virtue of being dead.

So within this context you may be surprised to find me writing about a young new performer who has recently appeared on the scene—one whose abilities are extraordinary. Every show has people walking away with broad smiles and looking visibly moved.

The show itself is surprisingly static but rarely fails to be noticed and enjoyed. And it doesn't take place on a stage either. The venue is the street, always the same street and the same location. Those who come across this quiet showman tend to find themselves stopping midstride to look and wonder. Even people already acquainted with the performance will often stop to spend a few minutes or simply feel the benefits of having their steps lightened and their spirits lifted as they go by.

A QUICK LIST OF THIS YOUNG PERFORMER'S TRAITS

The performer or performance is:

- Unexpected
- Appealing to all generations
- The right thing in the right place at the right time
- Kind and comforting. Yet what comes out is sometimes shocking, sad or hilariously funny.
- Real value. Everyone, it seems, walks away positively enriched by the experience.
- Well defined and always on
- Great-looking and wears a cute hat
- Uplifting

Astute readers will by now have guessed, from the lack of personal pronouns in the above, that something is afoot. And you're right. Did you believe for a moment I was going to give a *human* performer some free publicity? Ha!

I am talking about a clever creation that has popped up on our street called the Little Free Library. The concept is simple enough. The library is a cute and well-made box with glass-fronted doors revealing several bookshelves (the lowest shelves are for children's books). A sign on the library invites passers-by to take a book and leave a book in return. It's really more of a book exchange than a library, but let's not quibble.

Setting it up was the work of my neighbour Theresa, and frankly I was wary of the concept. Having such a thing on a downtown street seems an open invitation to vandalism and theft and also offers rich possibility for unseemly and unhygienic objects, besides books, to be deposited on its neat little shelves.

But the other day, as I trimmed the yew hedges out front of our community, I noticed people going by with smiles on their faces. It didn't take long to realize that the transformative effect was being produced by the Little

Free Library. As my electric shears clacked away at the hedge, I observed nearly every passer-by stopping to check out the library. Most of them opened the doors to take a peek inside. Some people took a book. Not everyone *left* a book, but I had the feeling they'd soon be back to return the favour. My neighbour's kids came down the steps to return books they'd read and to see what new offerings were in store. The feeling of delight was palpable. I have rarely in my life seen such a simple object create such universal joy.

As an entertainer I couldn't help but be impressed by the profound abilities of the library to touch so many different people. And I realized that any of us with ambition to entertain others can learn a lot from this endearingly simple device:

- ***Be original, or at least be a new twist on a familiar theme.*** In this world of instant communication, everything is coming to resemble everything else. Only by spending time away from our screen devices and other distractions is there any hope of cultivating qualities such as uniqueness, character and style.
- ***Appeal to all generations.*** True entertainment is universal and has the potential to touch everyone.
- ***Be the right thing in the right place at the right time.*** Find the audience(s) and venue(s) that work for you.
- ***Be kind and comforting, but don't be afraid to occasionally be shocking, sad or hilariously funny.*** In this crazy and jarring world, people welcome gentle and soothing experiences. But within that established framework, find ways to surprise their minds.
- ***Give people a sense of having received real value.*** Just as every great educator is also an entertainer, the reverse is also true. What do people learn and take away from your performance? How will they be changed?
- ***Define your stage character (how you look, speak and move) as clearly as possible.*** Make yourself appealing to others and live in that mode for the duration of the performance.

- ***Look great.*** Exactly how you dress up will depend on your performance character, but wear something that sets you apart from the audience and tells everyone that something special is in store. A hat should look good and serve a purpose (see also page 132): the Little Free Library has a precious little shingled roof, making it look like a mini house while at the same time keeping the valuable contents nice and dry.
- ***Uplift hearts.*** Who doesn't want an experience where you walk away feeling that there is hope for us all, that good people will one day be in charge and that maybe, just maybe, there is more glory and beauty in this world than we ever dared to imagine.

THIS IS HOW LONG IT TAKES TO GET GOOD

Just like the kids who ask, "Are we there yet?" novice ukulele strummers want to know, "How much longer before I'm a really good player?"

IT'S NOT UNUSUAL, especially in North America, for a beginner player to be encouraged with spirited cheers, high-fives and *Way to go!*s simply for having made it from one end of a tune to the other. With all this praise from friends, family, teachers and peers, it's easy for new players to believe that if their improvement continues at the current rate, they will soon become a headline act.

Well, let me put you right.

Where are we really at in our progress? New musicians should indeed be encouraged with positive feedback and not be constantly reminded that they are at the beginning of a *very* long road. It can be more than daunting to know the true distance to our destination: like the Himalayan Sherpa who never looks at the top of the mountain, we ultimately reach our goals by incremental steps. But we ought to have at least *some* idea of the extent of the task before us. In the back of his mind the Sherpa is fully aware that he is climbing a massive mountain. But are you?

The ukulele is touted as an easy instrument. And results seem to back this up. How many thousands, perhaps millions, of people have been thrilled to see how quickly they trained their fingers to change chords and strum out a song? With family and friends patting you on the back and telling you how great you're doing, you may soon start to believe that you're disproportionately better than you actually are.

This is a natural human trait called the Dunning-Kruger effect, named after two scientists who did an experiment getting people to perform tasks of logic and joke-telling. But the real experiment was that they got the participants to rate themselves on their own abilities. Time and again they discovered that novices consistently rated themselves far better at the tasks than they actually were. This explains the mind-blowingly large number of people who film their awful performances and put them up on YouTube for the world to see. "What were they thinking?" you wonder. Well, thanks to Dunning and Kruger, we now know they actually believed they were pretty good. Joe Plink might seem a bit of a hotshot player to himself and others in his ukulele club, but put him on a bigger stage, outside of his immediate and limited circle, and it turns out he is actually quite mediocre.

Sometime or another we're all victims of the Dunning-Kruger effect. It's what gives us the confidence to keep going. Inadequacy and self-doubt can be completely paralyzing, and the false feeling of being more expert than we actually are pushes us through difficult situations. It has been likened to the opposite of depression. Interestingly, experts, able to place themselves more accurately in a world context, tend to have a much truer picture of their own ability. The effect probably also explains why fourteen-year-olds think they know so much more about the world than their parents.

Here's what happens. People assume that the time it took to get from novice to amateur is about how long it takes to get from amateur to expert. This is so not the case. Let me put it this way: on a scale of 1 to 10, if learning to play the basics on a ukulele is a 3, then learning to be a ukulele performer who can consistently wow audiences is somewhere around 587.

That may not seem very encouraging, but it's a far truer perspective of what it takes to get good. When I teach at ukulele clubs and festival workshops, there is often someone at the end who shyly approaches me after everyone has gone away. In a quiet voice they admit that things started off quite well for them but now they can't seem to get anywhere, and the gulf dividing them musically from where they are now to where they want to be seems so great. They ask, "What advice can you give me?"

They are so humble and it is very touching. In that moment I always feel I have so little of substance to offer. The gulf is indeed great, the mountain is high and the ocean is deep, and there is so much farther to go than you can possibly imagine.

So don't think about all that—just keep your mind on what you need to learn right now. And when you ask, "Are we there yet, Ralph?" I'll say, "Yes, we are. Just a few more miles. Oooh! Look over there. Isn't that a lovely cow?"

HEY! LEAVE TINY TIM ALONE

I get somewhat irked by things said about Tiny Tim. And in this rant I just want to say, "Lay off him!"

THE 2015 RENO Ukulele Festival was better than ever. Doug Reynolds, the ambitious festival director, created an Ed Sullivan–style variety show that was performed in the Nugget Casino Show Lounge. Unless you're close to someone who has put on a festival or a major show, you probably have no idea of the work involved in pulling those things off. That Doug attempted both in the same weekend was ambitious to the point of folly, although he drastically increased his chances of success by having great help from volunteers, musicians and, in particular, his daughter Jessica, who is both a talented organizer and a gifted performer.

I really enjoyed the show. As well as ukulele performances from myself, Dominator, Ken Middleton, Michael Powers and Victor & Penny, Doug also brought in Jacques Simard—a Quebec magician who'd spent months creating a floating ukulele illusion that was quite breathtaking. Jacques also made Jessica appear from an empty cardboard box before making her levitate during a *Phantom of the Opera* sequence.

The show roughly followed the format of a mid-1960s *Ed Sullivan Show*, complete with ads for products such as washing powder and Alka-Seltzer. The goal was to recreate the feel of the show as if, say, there had ever been an all-ukulele episode. Playing the key part of Ed Sullivan was an impersonator called Tom LaGravinese. Tom had the look, the voice and the eerie ability to inhabit the persona of the dour TV star while improvising various bits of stage business. But Tom came with a bonus. Doug was delighted to learn that, among Tom's rich cast of characters, was Tiny Tim. Tom appeared as Tiny Tim for the finale of the show, when, to the music of "Tiptoe Through the Tulips," magician Jacques produced him from an empty trunk.

It was indeed a grand finale, I thought. Tom is somewhat shorter than the towering Tiny Tim but in all other respects, thanks to wig and prosthetic nose, he climbed out of that trunk looking and sounding as if Tiny Tim had been fully resurrected. Wonderful!

But, at the moment when Tiny Tim made his appearance, it struck me that the audience reaction was somewhat muted. I had expected a resounding roar of approval, first for the magic trick, and then in joyful recognition of the iconic figure who had just been brought back to life. The fact that I didn't hear such a roar got me thinking that the memory of Tiny Tim is not as beloved as it deserves to be.

And thinking about it further, I know this to be the case. Often at ukulele festivals, but other places too, when Tiny Tim is mentioned, someone will remark that he did a huge disservice to the ukulele. They say he single-handedly put an entire generation off the instrument, because millions of people came to associate ukulele playing with also being a weird freak. Whenever someone says this, I can only presume that the person has no idea about entertainment and what it takes to make it to the top as a performer.

Who said it was Tiny Tim's responsibility to further the popularity of the ukulele anyway? As far as I'm aware, that was never his motive or agenda. So by what measure can he possibly be held responsible for turning millions of born ukulele players away from ever picking up the instrument? If Tiny Tim put people off the ukulele, then it is only because they were a bunch of jeering group followers who were perhaps a little too lazy to think for themselves.

People can be such suckers. You see it in so many ways every day, all the time. I dare say that sports, politics, religion and nationalism all began as beautiful and indeed sacred ideals. But somehow along the way, a few manipulative people figured out ways to get huge numbers of other people to shut down the thinking part of their brain and go along with what they were being sold.

And it used to be that ukulele people were not like that. You always knew a ukulele person would be a cool, intelligent, fun person to know because they could think for themselves. And you knew this because the rest of the unthinking herd was blind to the ukulele. To most people the ukulele was not worthy of attention. This was not the fault of Tiny Tim or Lyle Ritz or Don Ho or George Formby or any other famous player. It was a sign of the times. Rock and roll was in and plinkety plink was out maan, I mean, waaay out.

So leave Tiny Tim alone. He was extraordinary. His overarching goal was to achieve fame, and in that he succeeded superlatively. Every part of his persona, every act and affectation—the ukulele carried in a shopping bag, the high voice, the long hair, the makeup, the suit, the blowing of kisses and the songs—was consciously added piece by piece to make him what he was. All of it was contrived towards his goal of becoming famous.

He put it all together and put himself out in the public realm until he succeeded. *That* is amazing. If you think it isn't, I invite you to go ahead. *You* create a captivating and original personality and live in it until you become a world-renowned star.

But it wasn't just a look. Tiny Tim was a magnificent performer. Numerous people have told me stories of seeing him live onstage in both large and small venues. They went to poke fun and jeer at him, but by show's end his dynamic performance had them standing on their chairs yelling "Tiny! Tiny!"

So stop blaming Tiny Tim for the fact that a whole generation ignored the ukulele. It's not his fault. It's the fault of lazy thinkers who go with the herd and who are too self-involved to look around and realize that what they believe is largely a pack of lies.

THE JAM MASTER

Most musicians are familiar with jamming. Steve McNie (pronounced Mick-NEE) has elevated this form of group playing to the level of an art form.

I ARRIVED AT THE first ever Canada Ukes Ukulele Festival (subtitled "Weekend at Ralph's") in Ontario in May 2015 knowing the festival would begin Friday night with a *three-hour jam session* led from the stage.

"That seems a little long," I thought.

As fun as they are, being trapped in a room where a jam has gone way past its "due date" is, for me, a dreary way to pass the time. But what I experienced was a ukulele jam that was both entertaining and enjoyable, while at the same time bringing out a level of cohesive musicality in the participants that I've never heard in all my years of attending music festivals.

Lifting an informal jam to the level of performance requires a particular set of well-honed skills, and I found myself studying the elements of Steve McNie's work that make it so frightfully good.

NO BOOKS

The first thing you notice is the big projection screen at the back of the room. There are no songbooks. A songbook has the advantage that you can take it anywhere, make notes in it, flip it open anytime and play your music any way you please. But for group playing, the projection screen has several advantages. First of all, before the jam occurs, Steve creates charts of well-chosen songs that show words and chords but also display key nuances of timing. He artfully manages this without making the charts look confusing and cluttered (an achievement you don't truly appreciate until you try to do it yourself).

Since we're reading from the screen all heads face upwards, which greatly improves the quality and uniformity of the sound. Everyone is able to follow Steve's crystal-clear direction, which would be difficult with eyes looking down into books. Intros, endings and cut-offs are crisp and sharp. Changes in dynamics, tone and style are communicated with simple gestures. All this is able to happen because everyone is literally reading from the same page.

FAMILIARIZATION WITH THE SONG

Getting scores of ukulele players of all abilities to play an informal song that hangs together like a rehearsed piece is achieved by first workshopping the trickier parts of the song. This includes getting familiar with the start and the end of the song as well as running any chordal or rhythmic parts that may trip people up. But it also means spending some time "looping" certain sequences so that everyone gets familiar with the feel and pace of each song before it begins. Steve infects everyone with his obvious love of the music as we find the groove and sit there for a while playing a sweet chord sequence over and over again, as our ears and bodies all synchronize with one another.

ADDITION OF EAR CANDY

Steve is immensely musical (he's trained in cello and accordion), and he shares his relish of certain chords and chord changes that are like nectar to the ears. He often makes chord adjustments to songs by replacing the original chord with, say, a minor or major seventh that he deems to sound particularly sweet on ukulele. Attention is also paid to the quality of the singing, and basic harmonies are quickly taught and encouraged.

BENEVOLENT DICTATORSHIP

Making it all work requires focus from everyone, and Steve happily admits that his approach is somewhat dictatorial. But it's a very good-natured sort of dictatorship. First of all, the soft quality of his voice makes the instruction come across as soothing and kind. With only gentle pressure and no hard words, you automatically want to do as he says. The instruction is clear, focused and efficient, while maintaining a bubbling sense of humour and fun.

GENTLE DISCIPLINE

Before I ever met Steve, I'd heard that his jams have a "no-noodling" rule. Noodling is a term for playing your instrument when your attention ought to be elsewhere—such as listening to someone onstage. But if it is a rule, I never heard it invoked. Only a few times did he politely ask us to refrain from playing while instruction was being given, "because it will sound better if we all play it together."

UNITY

Every song began out of silence (rare to the point of non-existence at all other ukulele meet-ups) and finished with a clear and unified ending. The theatre's professional sound technicians, who are used to audiences who sing out of tune and who can't even clap in time, spoke of their amazement at the exceptional sound made by so many people. Admittedly, this was partly due to the large number of players who regularly attend Steve's weekly jams and classes and who've become more skilled and cohesive than any large group of (mostly) baby boomers have a right to be.

Steve makes the process of "getting good" at a song a complete joy, and the results speak for themselves. My only regret about his work is that so few people outside of Toronto get a chance to experience what I now think of as the ultimate jam. Talking to him later, I suggested he offer some version of the Steve McNie ukulele jam at other festivals. So if you're involved with a club or festival, why not think about coaxing him away from Toronto for a while? Or, if you're ever in Ontario, Canada, head on over to one of his jams and check it out for yourself.

PLAYING BY EAR WITH CHALMERS DOANE

Which is the superior skill: reading music or playing by ear?

NEAR THE END of October 2013, a van traversed a section of Nova Scotia from Liverpool to Truro—a journey of about two hours. The van contained a double bass, a marimba, a clarinet, an electric violin, two suitcases, four ukuleles, a bag full of songs and me. This van, with its motley musical contents, was driven by Chalmers Doane. It was my second weekend in a row in Chalmers' company. Having already taught at James Hill's Langley Ukulele Workshop in the west, we were now barrelling along an east coast highway after performing at Nova Scotia's Ukulele Ceilidh.

Chalmers can't help himself. His need to teach music is a compulsion that has been with him for at least fifty years. He took on music education as his life's work in his twenties and never quit. Not even in his time off, and while driving a van, does he stop telling stories from his life in music.

This is by no means a tiresome trait. Chalmers knows that to teach you also have to entertain. So for me, listening to him, while gazing through the windshield at the road ahead, beats any Hollywood movie.

Chalmers talked about a time when he was helping to prepare the curriculum for a university music education program. One enthusiastic colleague had been busy getting the program set up, and Chalmers was now invited to present his ideas to a faculty meeting. But there was a roadblock up ahead. The university professors had learned that Chalmers' curriculum included teaching all music students to play by ear. But the professors, disapproving of this plan, had the more elitist mandate of only teaching the students to read music. To their minds, playing by ear was not only an unnecessary skill, but one associated with distasteful and lowbrow styles of music such as blues, folk and (ugh) jazz.

Chalmers' colleague had warned him that his ideas about playing by ear were the reason he was now being called to a meeting with the professors. Because of his views, the program could be in danger of getting shut down. Chalmers responded, "They're not going to shut it down, because I'm right."

In the boardroom, Chalmers, ever the tactician, caught the professors off guard by skipping the perfunctory introductions and went straight into a story about a Stone Age musician.

"Let's call the musician Glonk. Way back before recorded history, Glonk's tribe would celebrate a kill with feasting and music. After the feast, while everyone was lying around scratching and burping, Glonk would bring out a hollow log, chosen for its pleasing sounds. Glonk played the log with two sticks: *dum-thad-dum-thad-rat-tat-tatoom.*

"Everyone loved Glonk's playing and certain tribe members noticed that Glonk was receiving special attention, including extra food and other favours. Realizing that clever use of the log could bestow similar rewards upon themselves, others asked Glonk, 'How do you do that?'

"Glonk replied, 'Man, you just do it like this: *dum-thad-dum-thad-rat-tat-tatoom.*'

" 'But *how* do you do that?!'

"Try as they might, they couldn't hit the log like Glonk. They begged to be shown how. So Glonk thought long and hard about the problem. Finally he came up with the idea of drawing some lines and dots in the dirt to describe the ways of hitting the log. Glonk said, 'Now, when I point to this line here, you hit the log there—that's your *dum.*' Having taught the others one beat, Glonk then pointed to a dot that represented *thad,* and soon they were playing *dum-thad-dum-thad.*

"And so began a turning point in music: it was the moment when music was no longer simply about hearing and feeling. It also became a response from brain to body in which the body was trained to react to visual stimuli. It was the beginning of *reading music.*

"The problem with this is that over time the people who couldn't play music got control of a system for teaching it. Furthermore, they got the respect of the general population *because they had studied.* These come-latelys, the ones who couldn't play, took over the business of teaching music while the real musicians, the ones gifted enough to make music without the aid of dots and lines, came to be unjustly regarded as a lower class of artist."

At this point Chalmers stopped and looked across the boardroom. "Now, gentlemen, what did you wish to talk to me about?"

A silence ensued as the professors pondered the significance of the tale. Chalmers acknowledged that, with his tactics, he'd deliberately caught the professors on their back feet, but continued:

"It is wonderful beyond words that we have the extraordinary music of Mozart, Sibelius, Chopin, Beethoven, Bach, Debussy and so many others, and quite right that students should learn to read and play their works. But we should also remember that every one of those composers played by ear. That is the real essence of being a musician. I've learned enough about the teaching and playing of music to know that I am right—that all music students should be taught to play by ear—and I thank you kindly for hearing me out."

So, how does this little story relate to ukulele players—a musical subset not exactly known for their elitist dedication to the classical oeuvre?

Most of us learn our songs with the aid of sheets of paper that show chords, words and sometimes notes. This is the most basic information needed to play a song. But to make your song swing, to make it hip and in the groove—in other words, to make music that people will love to hear—requires ear-playing ability. The nuances of the timing with which notes are played and the shades of how strings are strummed are everything. But little of that is written down—because you can't; it's too subtle and complex. You have to learn to hear, feel and play it for yourself.

And if something about the story of Glonk still niggles at you, perhaps causing you to mull over the possibility that the tale is not just about music but could equally apply to any discipline run by an elitist power structure—say, the professions of law, medicine and government, as well as education—then I suggest you get back to playing your ukulele. Sometimes it doesn't pay to think *too* much.

THE BEST UKULELE TEACHER OF ALL

Every ukulele teacher says their way of teaching is the best. Let's look at some popular methods to see which one is best for you.

UKULELE TEACHERS ARE no different from anyone else with goods or services to sell. The more they believe in their own product, the more likely the public will invest in it. That's why uke teachers will generally market their training techniques as "The best ukulele method out there!" And when I say "uke teachers," I am of course including myself in that category, because I've been guilty of such marketing too.

When it comes to marketing either my *Complete Ukulele Course* DVD series (note: blatant advertising) or my group workshops, I've tended to extol their advantages. For example, my DVD sales pitch might go something like this:

"With the DVD system you can choose whatever aspect of playing you wish to learn and observe it as many times as you wish. You get close-ups of what the hands are doing as well as hearing how it's supposed to sound. And the months of learning you get from an inexpensive disc is way more cost-effective than taking one-on-one lessons."

You can see in that pitch that while promoting the advantages of my own products I also, in a subtle way, put the student off trying other ways of learning—in this case, private lessons. Now that is all well and good when *I'm* doing it, but I have to say it's very naughty indeed when others do it at my expense. So perhaps we should all try to be fair and figure out what is truly best for the student's needs.

Here are some (I hope) unbiased thoughts on the more popular ukulele learning methods.

GROUP WORKSHOPS

Group workshops offer an inexpensive chance to learn a lot of stuff in a short amount of time. Often this can be from a top-level teacher who may otherwise be unavailable for private lessons. Such teachers (like myself) do not offer individual lessons but will teach workshops from time to time. A workshop may also be the only opportunity to learn from someone who normally lives geographically distant from you. It's worth bearing in mind that good workshop leaders are often entertainers too, which can make learning in a group setting both inspirational and fun.

Disadvantages include the possibility that you may become frustrated or bored if the workshop is not at your level. There also exists the chance that, through not getting much personal attention, you may miss a key piece of information and not even realize it.

INDIVIDUAL LESSONS (IN-PERSON OR BY SKYPE)

One-on-one lessons give you immediate feedback on whether you're playing a particular technique correctly. With a good teacher, you will get information and techniques that are applicable to where you're at right now as a player. Online lessons via Skype also mean that you are no longer confined to a teacher in your area, but can learn face to face from anyone in the world. In-person lessons, however, give you the bonus possibility of really getting to know your teacher. For example, my first stringed instrument was the five-string banjo. My teacher Sara Grey was (and still is) a working folksinger. The pleasure I got from hanging around with her and other musicians at their concerts was a huge influence on my future career choice.

An obvious disadvantage of the personal touch is the cost of paying for regular private lessons. Also some people mistake the act of taking lessons for actual progress. Meeting your teacher may be enjoyable social time, but without doing quality practice, it doesn't guarantee improvement. Sometimes an excellent musician can be an awful teacher and vice versa. So shop around and be ready to say goodbye and move on if you don't feel you're being given the instruction you need.

DVD VIDEO TUTORIALS

Video tutorials are good because you get to learn a wide range of specific playing techniques from a teacher you trust without ever leaving your home. This system gives you the ability to clearly see and hear what you need to do. You also get to rewind and go over things as often as you wish. You get all this for the low price of a DVD, so it's very cost-effective.

Disadvantages include the fact that this method won't work if you don't take the time to watch the DVD! I'm always interested to hear from people who work regularly with my DVDs or, conversely, those who bought one and never once tried it out. I wonder why that is. You'll need to develop self-awareness and self-criticism (which all musicians must learn) by listening to and watching yourself, because no one is there to give you feedback.

ONLINE VIDEO TUTORIALS

These are more or less free, which is a big plus—except for paying your Internet service fee, of course. Advantages and disadvantages are similar to those of DVDs. But whereas DVDs are more likely to be produced by experienced teachers, online lessons can come from anyone, so the quality of the teaching may be questionable and incomplete.

Subscription video tutorials are similar to the above, but you pay a monthly fee (usually around $5 to $20) to access a website that has video lessons from a teacher whose work you like. The cost at first may seem inexpensive, but over time the monthly $10 fee can add up to hundreds of dollars, so it's up to you to decide whether you're getting value for money.

LEARNING FROM FRIENDS

Spending time with others and sharing songs and techniques is fun and relatively cheap (depending how much you spend on food and beverages) and a fantastic way to learn. Ukulele clubs and other get-togethers are a great way to pick up new skills and get some friendly constructive criticism.

THE BEST TEACHER OF ALL

It's you. Every musical performer I've ever known has spent a great deal of time alone working at and thinking about how to get the most from their instrument. You are the one who has the ambition to play and entertain. Decide what *you* want to play, then figure out how to learn the techniques *you* need in order to express *your*self in the way *you* imagine *you* can. Use every teaching method within *your* time and budget. Try different teachers, try different videos. When a ukulele teacher comes to town, take advantage of their presence and participate in a workshop.

But then again, *you* may choose to go it alone, deciding instead to generate *your* own ways to play the sounds *you* hear—both on recordings and in your head. Doing so brings its own flavour of satisfaction.

You are in charge. *You* get to set *your* own goals and *you* get to do the work. *You* also get to reward *your*self for occasional successes and take pleasure in the daily routine of practice. And, since no one is judging you, *you* can do no wrong.

But if you're serious about wanting to play better, then *you* had better do something.

NOTES FROM A FIFTY-YEAR-OLD UKULELE ENTERTAINER

Where I share my thoughts and bare my soul on the hard reality of reaching my mid-century.

WHEN I TELL people I make my living as a ukulele entertainer, their next question is: "So what does your wife do?" When I report that my wife has not had a *paid* job since 1993, many people are floored and proffer effusive compliments about how amazing it is that I have supported my family by playing a ukulele for nearly twenty-five years.

As I turn fifty, I find myself looking back at the sort of entertainer I used to be in the early days. I'm not the same as I was. It happened slowly, and in increments, but for sure a lot has changed.

For one thing, I've become aware of how short life is. At this age I am realizing that there are things I will never get to do. The men in my family tended to live into their eighties, so I can reasonably expect another thirty years, give or take a few. This seems fine until you put it in terms of summers. I love summer, and this means I probably have only about thirty more summers to enjoy. They come and go so quickly. How best to spend the time I have left? Do I want to be entertaining at small gigs, festivals and market squares for the rest of my days, or are there other things to do?

Fifty finds me in a state of limbo. Do I still want to continue what I'm doing? In most senses I've become the level of performer I always wanted to be. It took far longer than I expected to get to this point, and the financial reward is less than anticipated—but I made it. So now what?

These days my drive to perform mainly comes from seeing the positive effect my work has on others. I don't learn new songs with quite the same gusto as I used to, and I rarely get the inner "high" that performing used to give me. In fact, I've reached a point where I could take or leave this career that I've built. I feel that so long as I can put some good in the world while having the chance to meet and amuse people, I could quite happily quit this musical treadmill and find some other job. But what would that look like?

Most of my university friends are looking forward to nice pensions. I, however, deliberately chose to live according to my own rules. I felt the changes within myself, learned new skills and then sussed out ways to leverage money out of my abilities. There's a scary component to knowing that I have to live this way for the rest of my life. But who knows, eventually all the little tricks I picked up from a lifetime of hustling for a living may ultimately give me an advantage over my friends, who will be relying on outside sources for their livelihood.

Everything in my career has trained me like a commando for what I do now. I'm a musical warrior; a strumming SAS combatant; a singing Navy Seal; a soldier of fun tunes; a one-man fighting force fully armed with instruments of distraction, capable of being sent into any stressful situation, prepared to disarm and amuse at a moment's notice, ready to free small groups of individuals from their fears and insecurities so they can take on life with a fresh outlook and a new perspective. I *could* quit, but what then?

I'm in good health and I have some great friends and a loving family. But aside from the basic needs of life, it's the knowing that there will be another performance up ahead that really keeps me going. With or without a ukulele, I will always be an entertainer. It's what I was put on earth to do.

So for now, since there are no job offers looming, and since I cannot imagine the job that would have me joyfully waking up at some ungodly hour of every day of every week, I suppose I'd better keep doing what I'm doing. Not only that, but I hereby pledge to keep getting better at it. So look out! There will be more surprises up ahead. And thanks for supporting my work by paying to come to my concerts and buying my books and albums and so on. This is much appreciated, and all I can say is "Thank you!"

But a pension would be nice too, so please let me know if you hear of anything. Meanwhile, happy birthday to me!

ABOUT THE AUTHOR

RALPH SHAW'S REPUTATION as a performer's performer is well earned. He has demonstrated his ability to entertain everyone from young to old repeatedly over twenty-five years of live concerts. Ralph's career highlights include solo appearances at major music festivals and collaborative projects with some of North America's finest musicians. In addition, his professional wisdom and his insight into what it takes to be a successful musical performer have made him a sought-after teacher for ukulele and performance workshops.

Ralph was born in Schefferville, Quebec, and grew up in Yorkshire, England before moving to Vancouver, Canada. He relocated back to Yorkshire in 2017. His background includes an early life by the windswept moors of the Penistone district, an applied physics degree from Liverpool Polytechnic, and a decade-long career as a professional clown and children's entertainer. Since 1997 he has been internationally known as Canada's "King of the Ukulele."

Ralph's other books, *The Ukulele Entertainer* (2011) and *Wings are Handy Things: And Other Flights of Fancy* (2023) are available from www.RalphShaw.co.uk, along with the CDs and DVDs listed below.

THE UKULELE ENTERTAINER

Powerful Pointers for Players and performers

ISBN 978-0-9732452-7-1

Print and e-book versions

"The collection of Ralph Shaw wisdom we've been waiting for ... from a true entertainer and a gifted teacher."— From the foreword by James Hill.

WINGS ARE HANDY THINGS

And Other Flights of Fancy

Print and e-book versions

In the third volume of the Ukulele Entertainer collection, Ralph eloquently uses his playing and touring experiences to reveal the laughter and learning, plus abject misery and anguish, that comes with a musical life.

LOVE (2013)

A collection of songs about every aspect of love: finding love, the exultation of falling in love, lost love, the comfort of a long-term relationship and the transcendence of eternal togetherness.

- *Produced by* Steve Dawson
- *Featuring* Ralph Shaw, Steve Dawson, Rob Becker, Chris Gestrin, James Hill, Anne Davison, Bria Skonberg, Christa Couture
- *Includes the songs* "Fair Kathryn," "The One Thing You Can Count On Is Love," "Golden Plover," "Avalon," "Fàce à Fàce," "Movie Stars, High Rollers and Big Shakers," "A Song to Bring Back Something Which Is Lost," "I Never Get the Blues," "I Love You Truly," "The One Thing (Reprise)," "The Way I Feel for You"

LAUGHTER (2013)

Covers subjects as diverse as conversing with dogs, the childhood friend who became handyman at the Mustang Ranch (Nevada's famous legalized brothel), the building of a ukulele case, the British vicar who got his legs waxed for charity, the art of learning to yodel, and more moments from Ralph's unusual life as Canada's "King of the Ukulele."

- *Produced by* Steve Dawson
- *Featuring* Ralph Shaw, Steve Dawson, Rob Becker, Chris Gestrin, CR Avery, Keegan Chen
- *Includes the songs* "Father David," "How to Build a Ukulele Case," "Greek Menu," "A Nice Cup of Tea," "I'm the Handy Man at the Mustang Ranch," "Everything Is Free," "Bird Lover," "Doggy Language," "My Yodel Teacher Told Me," "Meine Kleine Munchkin," "My Dog Rover"

BIRDS OF A FEATHER—UNPLUCKED! (2010 REISSUE)

Songs for children and families, including "The Galaxy Song," "My Favourite Things," "Dingle Dangle Scarecrow," "Lavender's Blue," "Movin' Day" and more...

BY GEORGE! (2005)

Classic songs from the George Formby catalogue: "When I'm Cleaning Windows," Leaning on a Lamppost," "With My Little Stick of Blackpool Rock" and more...

TABLE FOR TWO (2001)

Favourites from the 1940s such as "We Three," "Skylark," "Cocktails for Two" and "Lullaby of the Leaves," plus original songs "I Just Wish I Was in Love," "The Burglar," "Manikin Man" and more...

KING OF THE UKULELE (1998)

Hits of the 1920s, '30s and '40s. Includes "Puttin' on the Ritz," "Cheek to Cheek," "Paddlin Madelin Home," "Taking My Oyster for Walkies," "I Don't Want to Set the World on Fire" and more...

COMPLETE UKULELE COURSE DVD SERIES

THE COMPLETE UKULELE COURSE (2010 REISSUE)

Takes you from ukulele basics to learning numerous cool strumming styles you'll use forever.

UKULELE PLAY ALONG (2007)

Chord names are shown in the corner of your TV screen as you strum along with the twenty-six songs.

ESSENTIAL STRUMS FOR THE UKULELE (2005)

Learn samba, reggae, syncopated, bossa nova, swing, Bo Diddley, waltz and frailing. Includes lots of song examples and comes with a free chord chart.

THE COMPLETE UKULELE COURSE FOR KIDS (2004)

Gets kids strumming, chording, singing and having fun with a variety of songs.

Have a question or want to place a bulk order? Get in touch by email: RalphShawMusic@gmail.com.

INDEX

Printed in Great Britain
by Amazon

24741169R00126